Also Published by
NORTHERN ILLINOIS UNIVERSITY PRESS

HEARTLAND: *Poets of the Midwest*

Edited by Lucien Stryk

Contributors Are

ROBERT BLY
GWENDOLYN BROOKS
PAUL CARROLL
R. R. CUSCADEN
BRUCE CUTLER
FREDERICK ECKMAN
PAUL ENGLE
DAVE ETTER
ISABELLA GARDNER
JAMES HEARST
ROBERT HUFF
JOHN KNOEPFLE
JOSEPH LANGLAND
JOHN LOGAN
THOMAS MCGRATH
PARM MAYER
LISEL MUELLER
JOHN F. NIMS
MARY OLIVER
ELDER OLSON
RAYMOND ROSELIEP
DENNIS SCHMITZ
KARL SHAPIRO
WILLIAM STAFFORD
ROBERT SWARD
JAMES TATE
CHAD WALSH
JOHN WOODS
JAMES WRIGHT

HEARTLAND II
Poets of the Midwest ⤚ॄ

HEARTLAND II

Poets of the Midwest ⁊

Edited by LUCIEN STRYK

NORTHERN ILLINOIS UNIVERSITY PRESS
DE KALB   1975

Library of Congress Cataloging in Publication Data
Main entry under title:
Heartland II: Poets of the Midwest.
 1. American poetry—Middle West. 2. American
poetry—20th century. I. Stryk, Lucien.
PS563.H37 811'.5'408 74-12817
ISBN 0-87580-050-5
ISBN 0-87580-517-5 pbk.

ACKNOWLEDGMENTS

The American Review, for Gary Gildner's "Touring the Hawkeye State" and
David Ray's "The Blue Duck." *Anglo-Welsh Review*, for Stephen Tudor's "The
Augur." *Apple*, for Jenne' Andrews's "Words from Storms and Geese in the
Morning." Atheneum Publishers, for Marvin Bell's "About That" and "From
a Distance," from *Residue of Song* by Marvin Bell, copyright 1974 by Marvin
Bell. The Baleen Press, for Ralph J. Mills, Jr.'s "Door to the Sun," from *Door
to the Sun: Poems* by Ralph J. Mills, Jr., copyright 1974. *Beloit Poetry Journal*, for
Robert L. McRoberts's "Poem for My Students." The Best Cellar Press, for
David Curry's "I am of These" and "Thinking Back Seven Years and Being
Here Now," from *Theatre*, by David Curry, copyright 1973 by David Curry.
BkMk Press, for David Ray's "The Blue Duck," "Ravenna," and "Stopping
near Highway 80," from *A Hill in Oklahoma* by David Ray, copyright 1972 by
David Ray. Black Bear Press, for R. P. Dickey's "Humidity," "Shazam," and
"X," from *Concise Dictionary of Lead River, Mo.* by R. P. Dickey, copyright 1972
by R. P. Dickey. *Black Flag*, for Tom Hennen's "Minneapolis" and "The New
Arm." Broadside Press, for Walter Bradford's "T.C.," from *Broadside No. 31*,
copyright 1969 by Walter Bradford. Candlelight Press, for Marcia Lee Mas-
ters's "Figure," "The House in Chicago," and "The Man, My Father," from
Intent on Earth by Marcia Lee Masters, copyright 1965 by Marcia Lee Masters

Schmid. *The Carleton Miscellany*, for Greg Kuzma's "Greens." *Carolina Quarterly*, for Peter Cooley's "The Revenant." *Chicago Express* (Shoestring Publishing Corp.), for Peter Michelson's "Parable for Our Time." *Choice*, for James Bonk's "Elegy for a Polish Grandaunt." *Compass Review*, for Felix Pollak's "Nofretete." *The Cottonwood Review*, for A. A. Dewey's "The Blizzard." *Crazy Horse*, for Stephen Dunn's "Giraffes: The American Version." *The Critic*, for James Bonk's "Painting an Old Apartment." The Cummington Press, for Warren Slesinger's "Field with Figurations," "The Green Beginning," "Passage," and "Pine Needles," from *Field with Figurations* by Warren Slesinger, reprinted by permission of the author and The Cummington Press. The Elizabeth Press, for John Judson's "Finding Words in Winter," from *Finding Words in Winter* by John Judson, copyright 1973 by John Judson, originally published by The Elizabeth Press and reprinted by their permission. Epoch, for Warren Slesinger's "Lost Country." Fiddlehead Poetry Books, for Robert Flanagan's "Atlas" and "Heirloom," from *The Full Round* by Robert Flanagan, reprinted by permission of the author and publisher. *Fine Arts Calendar*, for Felix Pollak's "Historical Society Exhibit: Old Programme." *Folio*, for Warren Woessner's "Navajo Poem." *Foxfire*, for Warren Woessner's "Flitcraft's Woods." *Granite*, for Doug Flaherty's "Coming on to Winter." *Green River Review*, for James Tipton's "February I Turn Off the Porch Light and Go Outside." *Hearse*, for James Tipton's "Exit, Pursued by a Bear." *The Hiram Poetry Review*, for Franklin Brainard's "Inland Sea." Hopwood Committee, University of Michigan, for James B. Allen's "The Homecoming" and "Night Shift in the Plating Division of Keeler Brass" and Linda Parker-Silverman's "Nursing Home" and "Advice to the Lovelorn." Ironwood Press, for G. E. Murray's "A Pavement Artist," "The Driving Wheels," and "The Plant Rhythms," from *A Mile Called Timothy* by G. E. Murray, copyright 1972 by G. E. Murray. Ithaca House, for James Bertolino's "Beyond the Storm," "Employed," "Eve of July Fourth," "The Marriage," and "The Red Dress," from *Employed* by James Bertolino, copyright 1972 by James Bertolino. *Kansas Quarterly*, for Norbert Krapf's "Darkness Comes to Woods," copyright 1974 by *Kansas Quarterly*. Konglomerati Press, for Mary Shumway's "Cattails for Bennett," "Firelocked," and "Flight," from *Time, and Other Birds* by Mary Shumway, reprinted by permission of the author and publisher. *The Lamp in the Spine*, for Jenne' Andrews's "In Pursuit of the Family." *Literata (Minnesota Daily)*, for Jenne' Andrews's "Sounding" and Louis Jenkins's "Library." *The Little Magazine*, for Jenne' Andrews's "Wife." *Little Square Review*, for George Chambers's "The Voice." Louisiana State University Press, for Stanley Plumly's "One Song," from *In the Outer Dark* by Stanley Plumly, 1970, reprinted by permission of the author and publisher. Macmillan Publishing Co., for Laurence Lieberman's "A Dream of Lakes," from *The Unblinding*, by Laurence Lieberman, reprinted with permission of Macmillan Publishing Co., Inc., copyright 1966 by Laurence Lieberman. *The Midwest Quarterly*, for Victor Contoski's "The Kansa." *Mikrokosmos*, for D. Clinton's "Breathing, at Last, in the Wichita Art Museum." *The Minnesota Review*, for James Bonk's "Acrophobe & Lapidary" and Harley Elliott's "Outside Abilene," copyright 1972 by New Rivers Press. *The Nation*, for Robert Dana's section 39 of "Natural Odes/American Elegies," which first appeared in *The Nation* under the title, "Christmas, 1972: The Gift of Fire," and Doug Flaherty's "Raspberries." *The New Laurel Review*, for Jim Barnes's "Year's End." *The New Republic*, for Peter Michelson's "When the Revolution Really," reprinted by permission of *The New Republic*, copyright 1973 by Harrison-Blaine of New Jersey, Inc. *The New York Quarterly*, for A. A. Dewey's "At the Drive-In: 'John Wayne vs. God.'" *The New York Times*, for Philip Dacey's "The Animals' Christmas" and David Allan Evans's "The Citizens' Complaint" and "Some Lines on the Razing of the Sioux City Armour's Plant." *North Country Anvil*, for Carl Rakosi's "The Old Codger's Lament." *Northeast*, for George Chambers's "The Life." Northeast/Juniper Books, for Robert Flanagan's "State Message: A Midwestern Small Town," from *News from a Backward State* by Robert Flanagan, reprinted by permission of the author and publisher. *The North Stone Review*, for Franklin Brainard's "Roubaix Cemetery." *Northwest Review*, for Albert Goldbarth's "Letter Back to Oregon" and William Stafford's remarks from his "On Being Local" (first printed in *Tennessee Poetry Journal*), quoted in the editor's Introduction, reprinted by permission of *Northwest Review* and William Stafford. One, for Tom Hennen's "Smelling a Stone in the Middle of Winter." *Panache*, for A. G. Sobin's "March Rite: Getting it Up." *Pebble*, for James Tipton's "Winter in Elwell." Permanent Press, for Robert Vas Dias's "Petoskey Stone," copyright 1972 by Robert Vas Dias. *Perspective*, for Franklin Brainard's "Raingatherer." University of Pittsburgh Press, for Jon Anderson's "Stories," reprinted from *In Sepia* by Jon Anderson, by permission of the University of Pittsburgh Press, copyright © 1974 by the University of Pittsburgh Press. *Poem*, for Jim Barnes's "A Sunday Dreamer's Guide to Yarrow, Missouri." *Poetry*, for Michael Heffernan's "A Figure of Plain Force" and "The Apparition," copyright 1972 by the Modern Poetry Association; Greg Kuzma's "Melons" and "The Weak," copyright 1974 by the Modern Poetry Association; Marcia Lee Masters's "Figure" and "The House in Chicago," copyright 1963 and 1958 respectively by the Modern Poetry Association; and A. G. Sobin's "The January Sky," copyright 1974 by the Modern Poetry Association. *Poetry Northwest*, for John Judson's "24 December." *Poetry Now*, for Dan Gerber's "Homecoming," "The Line," and "The Tragedy of Action" and James Tipton's "Now Everyone Is Writing Poems about Indians." *Poetry Review*, for Robert Vas Dias's "Salvaging Spikes." *Preview*, for Louis Jenkins's "Medicine." *Red River Valley Historian*, for Richard Lyons's "Medora, N.D." *River Bottom*, for Greg Kuzma's "Garden Report." Scopcraeft Press, for Bruce Severy's "Crossing into the Prairies," from *Crossing into the Prairies* by Bruce Severy, copyright 1973 by Scopcraeft Press. *Shenandoah*, for Peter Cooley's "Tracks," copyright 1973 by *Shenandoah*, reprinted from *Shenandoah*: The Washington and Lee University Review with permission of the Editor; David Allan Evans's "Neighbors," copyright 1971 by *Shenandoah*, reprinted from *Shenandoah*: The Washington and Lee University Review with permission of the Editor; and Stanley Plumly's "Pull of the Earth," copyright 1972 by *Shenandoah*, reprinted from *Shenandoah*: The Washington and Lee University Review with permission of the Editor. *South Dakota Review*, for James Tipton's "Dialogue" and Mark Vinz's "For the Far Edge." *Sou'wester*, for Philip Dacey's "Anniversary" and Dave Smith's "High Are the Winter Rivers" and "Pietas: The Petrified Wood." *Southwest Review*, for James Reiss's "The Breathers." *The Straight Creek Journal*, for Tom Hennen's "Dirt Road" and "Going into the Woods." *The Strong Voice Voice III* (The Ashland Poetry Press), for Alberta Turner's "Wrists." *Sumac*, for Stanley Plumly's "Porches." The Sumac Press, for Jim Harrison's "I Was Proud . . ." and "Today We've Moved . . . ," from *Letters to Yesenin* by Jim Harrison, copyright 1973 by Jim Harrison, and Tom McKeown's "November on Lake Michigan," from *The Luminous Revolver* by Tom McKeown, copyright 1974 by Tom McKeown. *Today's Health*, for Franklin Brainard's "White Ropes." *Thrust*, for Ralph J. Mills, Jr.'s "The White Piano." *Voices*, for Marcia Lee Masters's "The Man, My Father." *Wild Currants*, for Louis Jenkins's "Portage Poem." Yale University Press, for Michael Ryan's "Hitting Fungoes" and "Your Own Image," from *Threats Instead of Trees* by Michael Ryan, copyright 1974 by Michael Ryan.

To the Memory of
PARM MAYER
1915–1971
and
THOMAS JAMES
1946–1974
Poets of the Midwest

CONTENTS

INTRODUCTION

1

A small town street known for years reaches through the universe: to the eye alive *nothing* is without its wonder. Sherwood Anderson knew this, and he set about creating a truer kind of fiction, as did—chiefly through his example—William Faulkner. And in poetry such was the achievement of Edgar Lee Masters, Vachel Lindsay, Carl Sandburg, and a few others. Before such art can come, however, there has to be a very strong spirit of acceptance, a love of life in its humblest manifestations and, conscious or not, a philosophical approach to the whole, hard won and hard kept. Here is William Stafford, a contributor to the first *Heartland* (1967), in a statement, "On Being Local," in a 1973 issue of *Northwest Review* (first printed in the now defunct *Tennessee Poetry Journal*):

All events and experiences are local, somewhere. And—all human enhancements of events and experiences—all the arts—are regional in the sense that they derive from immediate relation to felt life. It is this immediacy that distinguishes art. And paradoxically the more local the feeling in art, the more all people can share it; for that vivid encounter with the stuff of the world is our common ground. Artists, knowing this mutual enrichment that extends everywhere, can act, and praise, and criticize, as insiders—the means of art is the life of all people. And that life grows and improves by being shared. Hence, it is good to welcome any region you live in or come to or think of, for that is where life happens to be, right where you are.

But I had better begin by eating words (my own) from the Introduction to the first *Heartland*. I said, attempting to justify the comparatively small number of contributors, "I wanted especially to avoid the buckshot approach, single poems by numerous poets resulting in chaos, yet I am very much aware of the possibility that through ignorance or oversight I have not included work by poets the equal of any in the book."

LUCIEN STRYK / xvii

There were twenty-nine poets in that collection; there are more than twice that number in *Heartland* II, some of whom—among them the best known—have only a poem or two. The reason? After the publication of *Heartland* I became aware of my "ignorance or oversight," and knew that if given another chance I would bring in many more poets while avoiding, through careful editing, the "chaos" I had feared. Once again I am certain to have missed poets the equal of any in this collection, but do not feel that I have represented too few. When one considers that the Midwest is made up of twelve states, many populous, and each with its quota of poets, it becomes rather obvious that a fresh batch of talent exists for another *Heartland*.

Those invited to submit work were informed that I was interested in "chiefly unpublished . . . poems set in the Midwest, by writers from the area." I cannot guarantee that the book is without interlopers, but all were aware of the geographical limitations. There are a number of reasons for my having restricted the collection to work from or firmly associated with the Midwest, the foremost being that it was my intention, as in the case of the first volume, to give a full sense of the region. That in itself may call for explanation, especially in a time of intensifying international involvements. Although I am the first to admit that to be an effective writer a poet need not respond constantly to place and that there are some whose works do not in the least suggest where they happen to be produced, there is in the work of most good writers some sense of region, and often it is very strong. One reason for this is that the artist, as William Stafford suggests, invariably moves from the particular to the general, and though art is most convincing when it encompasses a great deal, a microcosm, it is always felt as such a process.

Yet there are some who would condemn, shrilly as crusaders, poems made in such a spirit, and there are among such detractors those whose will toward cosmopolitanism and sophistication is so intense that they do not appear to know where they live, outside the pages of slick magazines. The

Heartland poets, if nothing else, do know where they live and seem for the most part to be living integrated lives—though it is quite probable that on occasion they may have the usual misgivings—hankering for brighter climes, finding that they want to get away. Often, as might be expected, there is a breaking for the sea. Here is Laurence Lieberman, in "A Dream of Lakes":

Often as I troll rough waters
At sea, and haul in five pounds
Every minute on my shark-tested tackle

I feel like a man in a brothel
Who gave over a delicate catch
Or the intricate mysteries of search. . . .

And Judith Minty, in "Finding Roots":

Scavenged the beaches, sifted
through spindrift on salt-water shores,

put shells to my ear, heard
echoes, but never my name,
found bones of coral, fossils
that bore no family ties.

And so finished by turning
inland, ebbed back to the source. . . .

One falters, one snaps back to realities, the never less than wondrous particulars of a life, as Franklin Brainard, in "Inland Sea":

Here in the wind-shave of prairie land
through senses the animal did not think about
I feel the swell of seas
and in my mouth
waking
I taste salt.
My tiredness rises to a breaking.
I shall be coral for an unknown reef
of grass.
I shall be lime to green.
I shall yellow cactus flowers.
Because I live

because I love this living
because this animal would die to live
I'll die to rise again
as seasonal.
I shall be salt for absent Agassiz
lifting now to grass.

The gifted regional artist has always, everywhere, been the object of a special kind of sneering. Here is the British author Richard Aldington, writing awestruck in his *Life for Life's Sake* of Ezra Pound (the group of poets being disparaged is the Georgians of pre-World War I England, one detested by Pound and his circle):

The Georgians were regional in their outlook and in love with littleness. They took a little trip for a little weekend to a little cottage where they wrote a little poem on a little theme. Ezra was a citizen of the world, both mentally and in fact. He went off to Paris or Venice with vastly less fuss than a Georgian affronting the perils of the Cotswolds.

Aldington's contempt for those who might have found the Cotswolds (or Walden—what would he have thought of Thoreau?), or their own backyards, as interesting as a great city is not to be taken lightly—in spite of the fact that Thomas Hardy, say, with all his Georgian affinities is acknowledged to be a much more important poet than the sophisticates adored by Aldington. But could anyone really find praiseworthy the act of going off to Paris or Venice (with or without fuss), the sort of activity, doubtlessly agreeable, reserved for the privileged?

One wonders why such matters are brought up in the first place, what they have to do with the making of poems. Is it necessary to comment at all on the supposed superiority of one attitude or life-style to another? In order to appreciate the personal depths of Hardy's work in fiction and poetry, the powerful sense of a given place, is it necessary to question the inestimable achievements in technique, the native curiosity and openness to all aesthetic and philosophical possibilities, both Western and Oriental, of an Ezra Pound? I think not.

How can the range and degree of stimulations and influences ever be gauged? Who is to say that Hardy, a broadly learned man, was not in his own quiet way equally affected by other worlds? As evidence, there is that extraordinary epic-drama of the Napoleonic Wars, *The Dynasts*. The minds of most are closed to such possibilities, and it is much easier and more convenient for them to think in terms of opposing types constantly at odds with each other. They are admittedly helped along at times by the artists themselves. In his essay "Revolt Against the City," the midwestern painter Grant Wood (1891–1942) had this to say:

Occasionally I have been accused of being a flag-waver for my own part of the country. I do believe in the Middle West—in its people and in its art, and in the future of both—and this with no derogation to other sections. I believe in the Middle West in spite of abundant knowledge of its faults. Your true regionalist is not a mere eulogist; he may even be a severe critic. I believe in the regional movement in art and letters (comparatively new in the former though old in the latter); but I wish to place no narrow interpretation on such regionalism. There is, or at least there need be, no geography of the art mind or of artistic talent or appreciation. But . . . the fact of the revolt against the city is undeniable. Perhaps but few would concur with Thomas Jefferson's characterization of cities as "ulcers on the body politic"; but, for the moment at least, much of their lure is gone. Is this only a passing phase of abnormal times? Having at heart a deep desire for a widely diffused love for art among our whole people, I can only hope that the next few years may see a growth of non-urban and regional activity in the arts and letters.

Is it not possible to find the city richly exciting without feeling challenged by it, and that in the arts there is a "revolt" against it? I want to suggest through my selection of poems an urban/rural balance. There are certainly some very strong city poems, among them Albert Goldbarth's ambitious "Letter Back to Oregon," Peter Michelson's disturbing "When the Revolution Really," Keith Gunderson's "concrete" phalanx of "The Gypsy Motorcycle Club of South Minneapolis," and Walter Bradford's warm/tough realizations of ghetto Chicago—street people like T. C., Foster (a "pop-daddy" got by "the scag hero from the East"), and a "sweet city mama." And there are more, perhaps enough to make clear that the book does not have as one of its purposes the celebration of only farm and small town, at the expense of the metropolis. Nor does it understand nature to be found only in woods and fields. A modern reader need not be reminded that old divisions and categories are no longer to be taken seriously, that if at one time it was possible for men to see their world as separate town and country, the one hostile to all that was thought humane, the other sweet but rather empty, it is so no longer. Nature is everything and everywhere, and good artists find it.

Along with a distrust of the city there has been in the pronouncements of some regionalists a suspicion of the foreign: one's allegiances must be untainted. As one who has worked for a number of years, in Asia and the United States, on the translation and interpretation of Zen poetry, I am sometimes asked why in the face of such "exotic" pursuits I have an interest in the poetry of my region—or, worse, why my own poetry is set for the most part in small-town Illinois. To one involved in the study of a philosophy like Zen, the answer to such questions is not difficult: one writes of one's place because it is in every sense as wonderful as any other, whatever its topography and weathers, and because one cannot hope to discover oneself elsewhere. Of the three poems by Jim Harrison in this volume, one is a very personal response to the great Japanese Zen poet Shinkichi Takahashi; another—set firmly in the world of the poet's northern Michigan farm—is related to the astonishing Russian poet Yesenin. Here is how it begins:

Today we've moved back to the granary again and I've annointed the room with Petrouchka. Your story, I think. And music. That ends with you floating far above in St. Petersburg's blue winter air, shaking your fist among the fish and green horses, the diminutive yellow sun and a chicken playing the bass drum. Your sawdust is spilled and you are forever borne by air. A simple story.

A persistent, if not quixotic, intention of the *Heartland* collections is to help bring about a sense of community, through poetry, something I touched on in the Introduction to the first volume:

Planning the book, I felt that one of its most important purposes would be to offer proof that what appears to many a colorless region is to some rich, complicated, thrilling. That, in short, the Midwest is made up of the stuff of poetry. And once those living in it begin to see its details—cornfields, skyscrapers, small-town streets, whatever—with the help of their poets, they will find it not only possible to live with some measure of contentment among its particulars but even, miraculously, begin to love them and the poems they fill.

Preposterous as it may appear in these cynical times, I have in mind for the *Heartland* anthologies a uniquely spiritual purpose: to raise men to an awareness of the wonders around them, the perennial gift of poetry wherever it is made. As Walt Whitman, most hopeful and egalitarian of our poets, proclaimed in his Preface to *Leaves of Grass*, "The messages of great poets to each man and woman are, Come to us on equal terms, Only then can you understand us, We are no better than you, What we enclose you enclose, What we enjoy you may enjoy."

In various ways some have gone about trying, through poetry, to create a sense of community. In a 1974 issue of *American Poetry Review* (Vol. 3, No. 2) Robert Bly, a contributor to the first *Heartland*, describes his successful efforts to organize a cooperative publishing venture, the Minnesota Writers' Publishing House. As it develops there will be works produced from all over the state, and an anthology is being put together in which every county of the state will be represented. The writers hope to interest Minnesota high schools in extensive use of the book in the classroom. Robert Bly writes: "High school students, in our state at least, seem most astonished of all that poetry is written by people living in the Middle West, or 'in the sticks,' or in a small town, near them, or however they phrase their assumption that art is for someone else."

The feeling that art in the minds of most is "for someone else" was brought home forcefully some months ago when I was commissioned by the Illinois Arts Council to serve in a "Master Poets Program," the purpose of which was to train younger poets to be effective readers of their own work. I tried to interest a number of high schools in northern Illinois, explaining to principals and English department chairmen the purpose and scope of the program, as well as the responsibilities of those engaged in it. The program, funded by the National Endowment for the Arts, would be given without charge and would take up only two or three hours, apart from preparations made by the schools prior to the program—mimeographing and discussion of the poets' work, selection of some student poetry for analysis, and so forth. Feeling confident that with such inducements the response would be altogether positive, I sat back and waited. Of the thirty or more schools approached, only six accepted the programs. Those which did not thought presumably that they would be worthless, disruptive, or too much trouble, and most of their administrators did not even bother to decline in writing something so irrelevant to the purpose of education as the appreciation of poetry. The indifference suggested by such attitudes to the possibilities of poetry in the life of the young, and the inequity (where there was interest the students and teachers appeared to gain a great deal from the programs—people living around them whose poems did not deny the reality of their world) are very disturbing. The inescapably sinister conclusion is that too many persons in positions of responsibility seem to feel that poetry is "for someone else," an elitist art practiced by and meant for only the culturally privileged.

It is small wonder, then, that the *Heartland* poets, on the evidence of their work, feel more isolated (with all those Midwest miles between them) than poets elsewhere. Some of their work reminds one of those Chinese T'ang Dynasty poems written by men like Tu Fu and Li Po, who, after brief, infrequent encounters in their mountain retreats, drunk with wine and the poignancy of nearing departure, celebrated friendship and the art that sustained them. There are pieces in both *Heartland* volumes filled with such emotion, in which, as in John Judson's "24 December," "snow and the landscape's / clarity will keep us / this American distance / from each other"; and where, as in Peter Cooley's "Packer City Poem," we hear an occasional cry for succor: "Help, help, I'm up the middle / of middle america & can't break out." It is very close to the dominant mood in Edgar Lee Masters (about whom in the collection there are moving poems by his daughter Marcia Lee Masters), and many have gathered on the banks of his Spoon River. Thoreau, as usual, was right, for his New England was everywhere and forever:

The mass of men lead lives of quiet desperation. What is called resignation is confirmed desperation. From the desperate city you go into the desperate country, and have to console yourself with the bravery of minks and muskrats. A stereotyped but unconscious despair is concealed even under what are called the games and amusements of mankind.

This is illustrated quite aptly in James Wright's dark poem, "Autumn Begins in Martins Ferry, Ohio," included in the first *Heartland*.

In the Shreve High football stadium,
I think of Polacks nursing long beers in Tiltonsville,
And gray faces of Negroes in the blast furnace at Benwood,
And the ruptured night watchman of Wheeling Steel,
Dreaming of heroes.

All the proud fathers are ashamed to go home.
Their women cluck like starved pullets,
Dying for love.

Therefore,
Their sons grow suicidally beautiful
At the beginning of October,
And gallop terribly against each other's bodies.

There is some despair expressed in the poems here, but mainly just loneliness, which only those capable of feeling poetry — or the lack of it — around them can know. The best of the poets, and all of them at their best, reject bitterness. As Albert Camus says in "The Artist and His Time," "One of the temptations of the artist is to believe himself solitary, and in truth he hears this shouted at him with a certain base delight. But this is not true. He stands in the midst of all, in the same rank, neither higher nor lower, with all those who are working and struggling." It is unquestionably difficult, however, to accept indifference, and as Mark Vinz writes in "For the Far Edge":

No one will believe the poets —
poets singing in the sunflowers,
poets in buffalo robes
dancing on tiptoe in their own hair,
Martin Luther and Buddha
swimming naked in the Red River.

"No one will believe the poets." And Bruce Severy, who in "Talks with Himself" writes of having "no treasures to show / but spoil banks / of empty shotgun shells, / you own no land, / but sit in a borrowed outhouse / by the new highway / and lay down thoughts / like windrows," has to defend himself publicly, even in national weeklies, against the charge, leveled by townsmen in North Dakota, of teaching an immoral book—one which elsewhere wouldn't raise an eyebrow. It's a wonder they hang on, out there in the boondocks, wringing poems out of whatever they can, but they do, and are the better for it—even if at times they doubt themselves. When they have known something different, they occasionally write of it, as does Stephen Dunn in "The City Boy":

He lives near a grain elevator, farms
on all sides. Everyone knows his name.
Amazing! The stars get through to the eye
at night. He hasn't been afraid for a year.

But wherever he goes, a foreigner goes with him.
He stands on the flat land, unsure
of his balance. He dreams of his silhouette
stuck against the sky.

From his warm house in an immaculate season
he begins the poem again, the one
in which the city, coughing now,
gone to pieces, is forgotten.

It hangs on. It hangs on.

At their very best, the *Heartland* poets, as writers every-
where, write not of the problems of personal adjustment
but of other humans, sometimes warmly, sometimes crit-
ically—as men and women whose art has lifted them
above self. By poem after poem in this collection we are made
to share in the compassion for these people who are leading
lives of "quiet desperation," and it must be said that the
strongest poems are revelatory. I used this admittedly gen-
eral term elsewhere (in an interview in *Chicago Review* 88,
1973) when, in response to the interviewer's remark that art
must encompass an entire vision, or "show that moment
when an individual becomes aware that such a vision is pos-
sible," I stated,

. . . the vision is possible, there to be pursued . . . par-
taken of in greater measure. So the revelatory quality of art
would . . . point to a way of life. In other words . . . the
poet, once things have begun to reveal themselves . . .
once he begins writing well . . . wants more of the same;
he wants to engage more fully in this world . . . the things
that happen . . . are seen as never before. Thus it becomes
a kind of self-perpetuating process. Something is put into
motion. A poet is started. . . .

Choosing an example at random, from poems short enough
to quote in full (the collection has been put together, after all,
with such an ideal in mind), I feel Tom Hennen's "Old Folks
Home" will serve:

On shadowy back porches
Rocking chairs
Are still
As fallen trees.

The old
Are

Imprisoned
In those bomb shelters
I see on the edge
Of prairie towns.

Strapped down
For a long voyage
They can't tell us anything
But only orbit
Far out in the gloom
Forever.

3

Another point made in the Introduction to the first *Heartland*
and perhaps worth making again, considering its importance
to both books, is that using poems of midwesterners exclu-
sively makes possible the representation of some who have
had little or no prior publication, and whose only qualifica-
tions are their gifts. In standard anthologies offered by many
commercial houses, most of which are echoes of each other,
made up not only of the work of the same poets but, incredi-
bly, for the most part the very same poems, one does not
expect to find poets without impressive "credentials,"—
publication in prestigious periodicals, a book or two. Now
any anthology will have the work of some whose talents have
been acclaimed, and *Heartland* is no exception, but there is
also a fairly large group who have published hardly at all, or
only in the littlest of the "littles." A book like this would offer
little opportunity for discovery if one were obliged to choose
among safely established reputations: *Heartland II* has an en-
tirely new cast. It has given me a distinct kind of pleasure to
bring in lesser known poets, and I believe their poems to be
among the finest in the volume.

I feel so strongly about this that I have begun to imagine a
turnabout in the literary world, a conscious seeking on the
part of editors throughout the land, section by section, for
poets unrecognized because of laziness, insensitivity, and
mercantile fear of those in positions of influence, major pub-
lishers not excepted—recent announcements by some that

unsolicited manuscripts would no longer be read represent a
nadir in American culture. I certainly do not conceive of
Heartland as a harbor for the rejected, far from it, but as I write
I am reminded of the difficulties faced by one of the two poets
to whose memory this volume is dedicated, Parm Mayer.
Repeatedly his fellow poets have referred to his poems as
being among the outstanding contributions in the first collec-
tion; the poems are quirky, passionate, with an almost primi-
tive force—qualities that were appreciated by editors of some
of the finest periodicals, which published his work regularly.
"The Day I Lay Myself Down" begins:

> There were the knotted cries
> I had not heard in the beginning
> and the soft impact
> of watered-down requiem;
> the whacking of bone against bone,
> and a cave-cold dripping
> in what was left of hell.

And it ends:

> I said, Ha!
> And wrapped myself in a box
> of newly-sawed silence,
> exactly my size.

In his autobiography *Across Spoon River* (1936) Edgar Lee
Masters writes, "I feel that no poet in English or American
history had a harder life than mine was in the beginning at
Lewistown, among a people whose flesh and whose vibra-
tions were better calculated to poison, to pervert, and even to
kill a sensitive nature." Yet in only three years, 1935–1938,
Masters published a long autobiography, a novel, three biog-
raphies, and three books of poems. What would he have
thought if, like Parm Mayer, it had been impossible for him to
find a publisher for one fine volume of poetry? A poet exists
not only to express his "sensitive nature" among the hospita-
ble, or hostile, but to bring his work before the public. Why,
given Parm Mayer's undeniable gift, was *Heartland* his only
substantial appearance?

There is in Parm Mayer's work a marked regional quality, something shared by many in this volume, but I would be the last to refer to it as a *Heartland* quality. Indeed there are some differences in tone between the two *Heartland* collections, which after all are separated by eight years of the kinds of turmoil always found in the arts. In the first volume there were many more formal poems, written at a time when many of the modernists were inveighing against not only true formal poems but even against verse tipped slightly in that direction. I felt obliged to enter the arena:

Things have become very simple. Writing a certain kind of poem these days is like holding out the red cape, and since poets are rarely nimble on their feet, they are often gored. Of course it is always possible to become a cow.

Whether a poem is memorable or forgettable is still the only question worth asking. If unsuccessful "formal" poems resemble knocking engines, unsuccessful "free" poems are like trays of junk jewelry onto which, though not always, a few real gems have been dropped.

In the intervening years something, obviously, has happened. In this collection there are few formal poems, among them being Jim Barnes's piece about his students—surely a theme where formal treatment would be seen as appropriate. It is always unwise to speculate on these matters, but perhaps of some importance to the change in attitude, pronounced by any standards, concerning the very structure of poetry has been the interest in foreign verse, even the finest translations of which rarely convey an adequate sense of formal detail. A young man beginning in poetry, in the remotest corner of the Midwest, is as likely to pick up today a volume of translations—Rilke, Neruda, Montale—and get as much from the reading as from the work of Eliot, Pound, or Stevens, not to speak of the "Midland Triumvirate" of a generation ago. This tendency has been evident for some years, but the effects only recently—they are especially apparent to one gathering poems for a volume like this, and are both good and bad.

The range and swell of Theodore Roethke's "North American Sequence" in *The Far Field*, or the superb concisions of his earlier "greenhouse" poems, are unlikely to be matched in the translations of even the greatest moderns, and certainly in the work of many poets something close to "translationese" is seen. Still, few would deny the rich satisfactions of the best foreign poems, and why should one hover timorously over them out of some theoretical fear, thus cutting off a source of major creative growth? When the work of a foreign poet is not properly absorbed by the writer, there is strong likelihood that mere oddness will result, and—thinking of the quality of translations—some of the greatest poets, Rilke among them, have at times been poorly served, with damaging effect. A foreign poet is, after all, only as good as his best translator. Often foreign verse offers something altogether unique, as might be expected, and many of the poets in the collection have learned from the best of it. Without the example of the Surrealists, for example, I wonder if Nathan Whiting's "Good-By on an All Day Bean Planter" would have been written:

In my life there will be U.S. famine.
My strength has worked into the land.
My fertilizer neck.
My wood spray ears.
My bug killing toes are done.
The nation's energy has passed through me.
I piddled it out.
I lost a herd of steers
to an asbestos commercial.
I plowed the hill tops.
I hid a year's corn in a gopher
to plead bankruptcy.
Sell me to the labor exchange backwards
and feed my duck.

One thinks not only of Breton and Eluard, but of the miraculous journeys of poetry—from the terrace of a Parisian café to an Illinois soybean field.

There have been since the first *Heartland* other impressive developments in American poetry. The prose poem was written by very few when I was looking for poems for that volume, and in the Introduction I described Karl Shapiro's *The Bourgeois Poet*, a book made up entirely of prose poems, a few of which I used, as a breakthrough in verse. There were intemperate discussions of the book in journals of the period, some dismissing it altogether, others—particularly those aware of the distinguished history of the prose poem, from Baudelaire on—greeting it as something very healthy for American poetry: the attempt on the part of one of its chief makers to introduce something radically different. In the book itself, Shapiro did not mince words:

Why so much attention to the printed page, why the cosmetology of font and rule, meters laid on like fingernail enamel? Why those lisping indentations, Spanish question marks upside down? Why the attractive packaging of stanza? Those cartons so pretty, shall I open them up? Why the un-American-activity of the sonnet? Why must grown people listen to rhyme? How much longer the polite applause, the tickle in the throat?

It is immaterial that not long after those words were written Karl Shapiro returned to the sonnet with a vengeance, just as it is less important than some seem to think that Robert Lowell in recent work has returned to strict forms after the remarkable liberations of *Life Studies*. Such fluctuations of the spirit cannot be graphed by literary critics, and all such attempts represent a kind of amateur psychologizing. The main thing is that these journeys, however short, are carried on by others, as is the case with the prose poem, which, as genre, is abundant in the collection—in the work of Jim Harrison, Keith Gunderson, G. E. Murray, James Tipton, and Louis Jenkins, whose "A Quiet Place" goes:

I have come to understand my love for you. I came to you like a man, world weary, looking for a quiet place. The gas station and grocery store, the church, the abandoned school, a few old houses, the river with its cool shady spots, good fishing. How I've longed for a place like this! I've searched the country for months, years looking for just the right place. As soon as I got here I knew I'd found it. Tomorrow the set production crew and the film crew arrive. We can begin filming on Friday: the story of a man looking for a quiet place.

To what degree the casualness and the relaxed rhythms of the piece develop irony is hardly determinable, but one knows while moving through it that one is being asked to share a different kind of experience, not many removes, surely, from the sharply pointed parable or even the good joke—but something new and satisfying. And that, when it comes to technique, is what matters: something very special has been brought into American poetry by prose poets. There are some whose poems, if charting is necessary, fall between prose poetry and "conventional" poetry, Ted Kooser's "The Goldfish Floats" being typical:

The goldfish floats to the top of his life
and turns over, a shaving from somebody's hobby.
So it is that men die at the whims of great companies,
their neckties pulling them speechless into machines,
their wives finding them slumped in the shower
with their hearts blown open like boiler doors.
In the night, again and again these men float
to the tops of their dreams to drift back
to their desks in the morning. If you ask them,
they all would prefer to have died in their sleep.

There is bitter humor in such work, and, method aside, that is a quality common to this collection. Rarely does it reach the point of cynicism, which has nothing to do with poetry, but it is a tough vein, suggestive of realistic appraisals, aware of actualities. It is not the only form of humor, however—there is the poem, equally common, in which the object is as much sympathized with as mocked. Here is "Neighbors," a sharp portrait by D. A. Evans:

They live alone
together,

she with her wide hind
and bird face,
he with his hung belly
and crewcut.

They never talk
but keep busy.

Today they are
washing windows
(each window together)
she on the inside
he on the outside.
He squirts Windex
at her face;
she squirts Windex
at his face.

Now they are waving
to each other
with rags,

not smiling.

Or as E. E. Cummings once put it, "Life, for mostpeople,
simply isn't. . . . What do mostpeople mean by living?
They don't mean living . . . the tyranny conceived in mis-
conception and dedicated to the proposition that every man
is a woman and any woman is a king, hasn't a wheel to stand
on." The humor in "Neighbors" has some of the sophistica-
tion of Cummings (those first two lines), and is found
throughout the volume, in George Chambers, D. Clinton, R.
P. Dickey, Richard Lyons, Felix Pollak, Carl Rakosi, Michael
Ryan, David Steingass, James Tipton, and others—a persis-
tent strain, to say the least. But perhaps it is the other sort,
less sophisticated, harsher, at times downright crude, deriv-
ing in large measure from the example of men like Sandburg,
and very midwestern, which has the greater social purpose
(though by no means greater importance as poetry), a good
example being A. A. Dewey's "At the Drive-In":

The sound of faint thunder
was silenced by the volume
of his voice.

But black clouds rolled in;
lightning hit the power lines,
and John Wayne vanished.

God won,
and the red-necks

dumped the beer cans
and tore out in their
American-flagged pickups,
looking for some ass.

4

Responding in the first *Heartland* to a charge by John T.
Flanagan that midwestern writers "won distinction in spite of
their style rather than because of it. . . . the work . . . is
rarely aesthetically pleasing," I quoted from Sherwood An-
derson's "An Apology for Crudity" a passage of great in-
sight that ends with the question, "Why talk of intellectuali-
ty . . . when we have not accepted the life we have?" For a
very long time the life, and the language, we have was hardly
accepted. Louis Untermeyer describes in the preface to his
volume *Modern American Poetry* the response to the early
work of Sandburg:

When *Chicago Poems* first appeared, it was received with a
disfavor ranging from hesitant patronization to the scornful
jeers of the academicians. Sandburg was accused of verbal
anarchy; of a failure to distinguish prose matter from poetic
material; of uncouthness, vulgarity, assaults on the English
language and a score of other crimes.

This came years after Walt Whitman, the spirit behind the
verbal revolution in American poetry, wrote: "We must have
new words, new potentialities of speech—an American range
of self-expression. . . . The new times, the new people need
a tongue according, yes, and what is more, they will have
such a tongue—will not be satisfied until it is evolved."

Have the poets in this collection accepted the "life we
have," have they the "tongue" to convey adequately their
vision of it? That they have should be self-evident, but what
for the poets is the life we have? There are no easy answers. If
Hart Crane could write, in his essay "Modern Poetry," "For
unless poetry can absorb the machine, i.e., *acclimatize* it as
naturally and casually as trees, galleons, castles and all other
human associations of the past, then poetry has failed of its
full contemporary function," Robinson Jeffers, in the fore-

word to his *Selected Poetry*, could write—and mean every word of it, as his life-style certainly indicated—, "Prose can discuss matters of the moment; poetry must deal with things that a reader two thousand years away could understand and be moved by. . . . This excludes much of the circumstance of modern life, especially in the cities . . . forms of machinery . . . (which) are all ephemeral . . . they exist but will never exist again." Robinson Jeffers envisioned, in "November Surf," a future with "The cities gone down, the people fewer and the hawks more numerous."

Such polarities of attitude (inevitably, always, the "truth" is in the eye of the beholder) are of especial interest when one considers the problems of the day, including ecology—not the abstract Sunday newspaper supplement issue it was around the time of the first *Heartland*, but in its grittiest aspects at this very hour: strip mining or no, pulping forests or no, making sulphurous caldrons of lakes or no. What are our responsibilities to the earth itself, to those who will inherit it, to those like the Indians who hold it as sacred—and on the bloody evidence of Wounded Knee are willing no longer to suffer what we do to it and them? Lest we forget, and minimize, it was once possible, and not so long ago, to suppress as lewd and "uncivilized" the great generative corn dance of the Chippewas, a midwestern tribe. This desecration was grieved over not by a politician but, as might be expected, a poet, William Carlos Williams, in his *In the American Grain*, a book which records many such events. Williams speaks of "the niggardliness of our history, our stupidity, sluggishness of spirit, the falseness of our historical notes . . . the tenacity with which the fear still inspires laws, customs . . . while morals are deformed in the name of PURITY; till, in the confusion, almost nothing remains of the great American New World but a memory of the Indians."

Of all men, the poet is least likely to bear false witness, which is why there was no place for him in Plato's *Republic*, and, though often despised, he has always been believed. The poets most respected today, particularly by the young (which is what matters), and wherever they happen to live, are not shirkers. If at one time, for example, the Indian was something being chased across a movie screen or, perhaps worse, was the sociologist's stupefied case study, today—as the poems about him in this volume suggest—he is for the first time in our history a human whose past and aspirations for the future are given their due. If bad conscience will out, the one place to look for it is in the poem. Here is John Calvin Rezmerski's "Pettigrew Museum":

Somewhere in all this mess
things stacked up in cases
and outside of cases
upstairs or downstairs
I expect to find
Sitting Bull
preserved
in all his feathers, beads,
dentalium shells,
elkskin suit,
quill-embroidered,
buried under all the hatchets,
all the quartzite pipes,
sinew-stitched moccasins,
Dakota hymnals,
beadwork,
pipe bags.
Somewhere under there.
If I find him, I'll know
buried even farther down
minus his scalp
minus his bad arm
Little Crow is still trying
to tell us to go home.

5

The 200th Anniversary Edition of *Encyclopaedia Britannica*, published a few years ago, spoke of "a Midwest renaissance" in American poetry, "evidence for which was supplied by the appearance in 1967 of . . . *Heartland: Poets of the Midwest*." I am not sure that it has come about, or whether, if so, the appearance of the volume properly heralded it, but I have found it immensely heartening once again to discover in all corners of the region serious artists doing their best with what they have, engaging in "that vivid encounter with the stuff of the world." It is bound to continue, and there will be future books published from time to time to capture the Midwest spirit.

The work of these poets has had a deeply personal meaning, for nothing in my early life encouraged the acceptance of—finding value in—the things around me. Rather the contrary: the "ambitious" young man was a seeker who would rise above his environment and look down from the heights of achievement at all he had escaped from—the past, home. Thomas Wolfe found to his despair that "you can't go home again." Others are doomed to perpetual questing for something else without even making *that* discovery. There is a famous saying of the Zen master Ch'ing-yuan:

Before I had studied Zen I saw mountains as mountains, waters as waters. When I learned something of Zen, the mountains were no longer mountains, waters no longer waters. But now that I understand Zen, I am at peace with myself, seeing mountains again as mountains, waters as waters.

In a sense, all true men, not only poets and philosophers, come to the very same conclusion, for it is the only sane one. If one cannot find fulfillment in the world around one, wherever it happens to be, there is no hope.

Poetry of the kind that fills this book can point the way, for it is written, even when seemingly critical of place, in the spirit of acceptance. It asks the reader to look anew at the things he has taken for granted, or been led by his culture to disprize—to come to more than terms with them, to love them. Only when that is accomplished, the spirit of these poems insists, can he begin to feel the surge of poetry in all that makes up his world, and live like one for whom poems are written, the very reader the fine poets of *Heartland II* deserve.

LUCIEN STRYK

HEARTLAND II
Poets of the Midwest ❧

JAMES B. ALLEN *was born in Grand Rapids, Michigan, in 1931. He attended a private school and took his B.A. and M.A. degrees from the University of Michigan. He is currently working on a Ph.D. thesis on the "confessional poets." His work has appeared recently in* Anon, Occasional Lunch, *and* Ann Arbor Review. *The poems that follow are from "See the Lighthouse Burning," a 1973 Hopwood-winning manuscript.*

THE HOMECOMING

Now I come home to you,
Exiled in my army overcoat,
Brushing the snow of Missouri
From my sleeves.
Both of us come at night,
You to possess the earth,
I to renounce your claims on me.
Father, we travel as strangers
To the garden of white stones.
The city that you loved
Receives you honorably,
The faces of your friends are broken.
We travel together over city streets.
I have nothing to say.
My uniform is pressed,
My shoes polished,
I set the dial at loss.
When I leave the city,
There is only the snow falling.

NIGHT SHIFT AT THE PLATING DIVISION
OF KEELER BRASS

The secretaries drive by the factory
Dreaming of rich uncles.
Across the street at Charley's,
The bar is jammed.
The neon sign pops and blinks
Like a wounded eye.
The heat rises over Godfrey Street.
In the plating section at Keeler Brass,
The acid bubbles in the iron tanks.
I strip down to my shorts,
Pull on the rubber gloves,
And lift heavy racks into the tanks,
The tendons in my arms
Pulse at the wrists.
Old Dutch works beside me,
An Allegan farmer,
He milks twenty-five cows
Before he comes to work.
He knows that college kids are worthless,
And works to wear me down.
In the last aisle, he swings the brass
Before a giant fan, the sweat drying
On his face as the metal drips
And shines like gold.
He moves among the vats,
Dreaming of metallic women in wheatfields,
Humming like machines.
He glows like burnished metal.
I am tempted to push him in,
A huge brass-plated skeleton
Swinging before the fan.
Instead, I soap my acid burns in the shower,
And hit the street, deserted now
Except for an indian walking his dog.

MICHAEL ANANIA *was born in Omaha, Nebraska, in 1939, and attended the University of Nebraska, University of Omaha, and the State University of New York at Buffalo. He lives in Chicago and teaches at the University of Illinois at Chicago Circle. His work has appeared in many magazines, and he has published one volume of verse,* The Color of Dust, *and a chapbook,* Set/Sorts.

RETURN

I

The distance back is greater
each time we settle on the journey;

it is a game of chance, this play
of time against the lay of the land,

the hills stretched flat, wheatfields
spread thin, abrupt highway towns,

brief irregularities of line, sloped
now like telephone wires at the window.

II

How will it begin,
second by second,
the strum of a taut cord,
an accumulation swirling in,
late snow storm drifting long
shapes, snowfences bellying
like sails to its weight,
or built up day by day
like the glow of a glaze painting,
the light coming back through
layered strokes as luster
and curve from the still life's
expected oranges and bottles,

or raged up like silt and rubble
with spring floods.

III

We know so little of weight,
she said, since we've come
to believe in flight,
so casually, as though lift
could measure anything at all.
Go to the corner, watch your
shadow lengthen as you pass
the streetlight, edging into
the next darkness. You push
your own contingencies before
you, carry those distances, also.

RIVERSONG

The sunlight on the water,
landfall shadows, treeline
edging down the slow current.

This is the land I made for you
by hand, what was touched once
then misremembered into words,

place where the soil slips out
from under its trees, where
stiff weeds fall like rapids.

It is the made emblem of time,
that only, nothing we have,
nothing we have ever held,

and it is only my arrogance
that calls it mine, this press
of clay on clay, this sluice

for cattle pens and sewers.
So, sunlight yellows on water;
treeforms blacken at dusk.

"Meanwhile the voice continues,"
or several voices, mine, yours,
those others that slide beneath us

among catfish and bullheads
angling in the slime, water voices
that suck the current in and pump it out,

gills that speak back waters the river's
long swirl threads into oblivion,
and her voice somewhere in the rocky

watershed, as yet unformed, thrilling,
who speaks in tongues so quickly, child
at the sunny edge of constant snow.

REEVING

Tricks of the weather
or slights of memory,
another Sunday empty
of touch, so clear
this January seems like May.

Impositions of dead fathers,
their remaining tyrannies—
the Dutch-German I never knew
panning for gold or harrowing

South Dakota into dust, quick
flashes of amethyst across
the blackened winepress
when late sunlight reaches
my grandfather's cellar,
hard spring of plow seat,
the dying gambler in black
coughing into his cards
or oiling the blue sheen
of his stub revolver.

More, certainly, than is needed,
these insistent returns—
as though the flat of Nebraska
were closing like a hand,
the rivers we have lingered by
spilling out through life-line
and love-line, the lines
of fortune and trade,
the slough of old soil.

Only the dust of hands,
season on season, what
gathers in the boot of
an empty silo or sifts
into the widening lines
of a rough-cut floor,
gathered back to haze
the city in, salt streaks
across dry pavements,
winnowings of a long winter.

JON ANDERSON, *born in* 1940, *has taught at the University of Portland (Oregon) and Ohio University, and is now teaching at the University of Pittsburgh. In* Sepia, *published in the University of Pittsburgh's poetry series, is his third and most recent book.*

STORIES

> . . . *as in old journals, we come upon a story*
> *that seems our own, and speaks, then passes.*

This is a story declining, as landscape
    Into its elements.
You saw that, driving through the Midwest:

How at twilight certain trees, houses
    You pass, float
On a flat expansiveness—such plain

Seclusive bodies as the stages of memory
    That darken & go by.
Finally not much will have happened:

Some processions you can remember awhile
    Between which the land
Goes on, gliding without force toward
    Night & sleep.

                *

You were telling a story. The story
    You lived was not
The same, though both had a loveliness

Which was years. And in the middle years
    You lost your way.
All winter the rain fell evenly down

& spring was mild. Evenings you took
    Your time, walking,
Coming home. What couples you passed

Talked quietly; bodies incomplete by dark,
    Hands touching, they
Glided by. The stars turned slowly
    Their exclusive joy.

                    *

From your neighbor the night divides you,
    & from yourself.
There was a dark, exclusive joy: the past.

All you had earned was passage. Fixed
    Points, by which
You measured time, a gradual lassitude

Had overcome. You accustomed yourself
    To the night. By
Lamplight, or firelight, you read

Yourself to sleep. These were your dreams:
    The steady motions
Of ships or seasons, by which disquietude
    You woke & read.

                    *

You had forgotten the words you wanted to say.
    I think you lay
Too often on a woman's breast. Now you were

Like those women who gathered on the shore
    Watching the ships;
Those heroes, their husbands, rose distantly

& dissolved. All of your constancy, now,
  Was only longing.
Most of it speechless, though often you wrote

Long letters, specific & even-toned, filled
  With ambiguous yearnings
For the absolute. You wrote about your work,
  Your wife, your home.

                    *

How can I say this, only beginning to see
  Such understanding as
Can make you whole. These stories end, as

Always, in our gradual belief. They are
  The lands we live in,
The women we finally meet as friends,

The friends we overcome. We overcome
  Ourselves. The words
You wanted are that story we tell

Ourselves so often it is eventually real
  Or plain; so, much
The same measure, or passing of time,
  Where we dissolve.

JENNE' ANDREWS, *born in* 1948, *spent her girlhood in New Mexico and Colorado before migrating to the Midwest. She began publishing in "little magazines" in* 1970, *and her first book,* In Pursuit of the Family, *was published recently by the Minnesota Writers' Publishing House. She has read her work in the Minneapolis-Saint Paul area, and is poet-in-residence for the St. Paul public schools,* 1974–1975. ["Autumn Horses" is dedicated to Stephen.]

IN PURSUIT OF THE FAMILY

The t of the pole is someone
with folded arms, turning away,
rotated slowly into dark.

The t of the pole
is the family,
standing on end in its coffins,
tilting into nightfall,
casting shadows like ridges,
set into rock.

These lives pass beyond reach
while the fetal human sleeps
on its delicate stem.

Out of sleep
the infant pursues the family.
First the grandmother
recedes, across the stretch
of midwestern darkness;
a farm tool corroded by wind,
bent over like a wagon wheel
half-buried.

At dusk she stands
on the road
with her braid of cinnamon hair.
The wedding gown
is like a sail, a winding sheet,
a cloud moving
with the long poles
over the prairie.

And one pole
is the father
who greets snowfall on the mountains
standing in the bare yard
while inside the children dream
of Pentecost, the wife sleeps
near bottles, ashes,
uneaten food.
Later the daughter's masked body
rests briefly on his shrunken mouth,
is the last image
to leave the open eye.

The child wakes later
in a cold city
to pliant arms.
Drugged by the body's
sticky tallow,
the small face rising
from the damp hair.
Dreaming after love
of cattle frozen
against fences,
their chins buried in drifts;
of human forms
sculpted in ice.

In winter
the buildings fade

like chalk against the face
of sky and mountains.
Telephone poles slant
along the river,
become sentinels
flicking into absence,
bishops walking to mass.

Each pole is someone
with folded arms
rotated slowly beyond reach
into night, frost, and silence.

AUTUMN HORSES

Autumn swells over the land;
palomino oaks herd together
and red maples flicker near the river.

A wet season;
storms drift through the night
and sense of you comes early through dusk
of brief nearness,
with the quiet purity of rain standing on tin.

Remembering fall on Pennock Pass
in similar weather,
when grey mares came bounding
down the field
as if pursued,

we release the disarray
of both lives meeting
to the wild color behind the eyes.

It is a season of migratory joy —
the body burning,
flying horses.

WORDS FROM STORMS AND GEESE IN THE MORNING

Light falling into my kitchen —
at last I have part of the world
and owe nothing.
Red, brown, deep gold spices
sift through my hands
   a boy sits at the table
   a man waits at the table
to put his hands on me
when I am done.
I have a new voice —
deeper, and the laughter has
a deep tone, rich
with love for the earth
and for daily being.
The body grows honed
from good use—thick, green leaves
and cold apples.
Cups of cider,
red berries in a brown pitcher.
After I move slowly with my
visitor, in the room I made
to seem like dreaming,
I will be alone. It will be good
to restore the place of things,
smooth over the quilt,
have a cup of tea
to begin the songs of reflection.
I think that my own company
is not so bad
before the snow flies

and that from my center
comes wide and blessed loving.
Something has come to be
in the grey tar paper house,
with morning glories,
a Cherokee landlord
and friends who disbelieve
harmlessly.

THE REACH OF WINTER

In the North
winter continues.
Friends are snowed in on Minnesota farms,
dreaming of Russian plains.
We welcome the fifth month of cold
in ice on the pail, no water,
a recovery of necessities
nearly forgotten
that wake an old motion in our lives
before cities
when like birds, we hardened
in making the year meet us.

This unending reach of wind and snow
can only be answered
by dreams of escape, conspiracy,
or finding new eyes in the night.
It becomes necessary
to make all the days into battlefronts
with the nature of things beginning.
The finish
is unimportant.

WIFE

After the cracked screams
of our argument
we sit waiting.
The day goes on without harder noise
than the soft rush through the walls
of cars passing;
of the dogs turning over in their sleep.
You have asked me about silence;
how to make decisions, muzzle creditors.
I can think only of things to eat
and speak to you of supper.
But silent in your chair
you are dim with shadows
wanting me to die, leave
or hold you.

SOUNDING

We have turned together
as if we made a slow tributary.
Before sleep
your glances were like brilliant wings
passing through the brush.

Now the sleeves of rain
drift off to other valleys.
A gull cries out
to test the river's distance.

We separate.
Musk rises from our bodies
and the damp trees
as our substance dries
into a continent between us.

JIM BARNES, *born in 1933, is currently an assistant professor of comparative literature at Northeast Missouri State University. His poems have appeared in* Poetry Northwest, Prairie Schooner, Concerning Poetry, *and other magazines. One-eighth Choctaw, he is scheduled to have poems in the forthcoming Harper & Row anthology* Carriers of the Dream Wheel. *He lives with his wife Carolyn and their two children in Macon, Missouri.* [The first poem here is dedicated to Brian and Sharon Bedard.]

A SUNDAY DREAMER'S GUIDE TO YARROW, MISSOURI

The town is tilted toward the stream,
oblique as shadows toward twilight.
But only the stream is on the move.
No wind to shake the rusty leaves
off trees that have never known a spring.

Standing on the bridge, you think the town
a creeper, some gray vine, thirsting
after a force to drive it home
into the hill.

       And on the hill
all the houses are asleep, or dead.
Rainbo Bread is basic metal now,
and Stamper Feeds has only ghosts
of gears. You want a flight of birds.

Yarrow was once a flowered town;
you think of mint. There is no one
to ask, no one to tell you now
where forebears lie.

       There are echoes
you are afraid to hear. You look
hard into the water and put a leaf
lightly against an eyelid to see

who is in your thoughts. A vision
dances on the skin: it is you,
the dancer and the dance.

On the hill
a last fresh grave blooms prismatic
in its finality.

YEAR'S END

Clouds prophesy; the sky portends
A flood. My mind's a thousand webs
Punctured by poetry and trends,
Current stuff. Thank God winter ebbs
And dies. The semester is gone,
Dead as Dante and Calderon.

Irony: a literary spring.
Students rebel; the long year ends.
Doting professors fly to Spain.
The pool is closed. A gardener bends
To pick a pod of paper from
A daisy basket, with aplomb.

My students did not see the truth;
They saw one another and chewed gum.
My fault. And I admit that both
Pride and arrogance struck me dumb,
And hot pants and the bra-less look.
Dactylic hexameter had no luck:

I gave them Homer, heroic deeds.
They preferred travel and communes.
I read them Lucretius, his seeds
Of things. I tried to teach them runes,
Shadow and substance, and symmetry
From Gilgamesh to Ted Roethke.

I figure up my retirement
And think of moving out of state.
Owls hoot. My head is hard as flint.
Sweating and several days too late,
I check an error, then remind
Myself it's glasses or go blind.

All agree spring's a time for love.
My students know, going with the sun.
I too feel it is time to move,
But feel is all I can. They run
Through more than books to make them wise:
A stretch of sand, laughter, night skies.

MARVIN BELL, *born in* 1937, *has lived in upstate New York, Chicago, Indianapolis, northern California, Vermont, Mexico, and Iowa City—where he teaches at the University of Iowa. His poems have won the Lamont Award, from the Academy of American Poets; the Bess Hokin Award, from* Poetry; *and an Emily Clark Balch Prize, from* Virginia Quarterly Review. *His books are* A Probable Volume of Dreams, The Escape into You, *and* Residue of Song. ["From a Distance" is dedicated to his father.]

FROM A DISTANCE

The tree will not ask for relief
though covered by sores and parasites
and misunderstood for a very long time.
Our shelled acorns and scalloped ivy,
our aromatic mint—trodden sentry—
are but underfooting for the wafer-
thin and hollow-needled snow

already bowing toward us under pressure
of a wet summer. An "early Iowa winter scene"
resembles a body, exquisitely blemished,
not lying but reclining as if modeling,
looking neither to the East nor the West,
and strangely! holding in place these shorn trees
we had passed by the mile without thankfulness.

But that is all changed. We lived on "the Island"—
New York's peninsular duck farm—
where the isolate fish-crow in the pine
gave a robber's thanks, and flew like a gash
through the air for the eggs of the others.
We were as far from the cities as I am from you,
which is not so far, Father, as you are from me.

ABOUT THAT

Love sells off a wilderness in which
blindness is a sort of marshy duty
and a weedy wrestle in all seasons.
Through dry eyes, it wasn't France,
but Montreal. The roads wound easily
to *Mont Royal*, the mountain sat ringed
by worn color, and the ringing just rang

and rang (echoes of missed ethics).
One might survive after all, it can
even be said you supped to suffer
on the word "delectable," which she was.
There is the nervousness of parchment,
and a haughty anxiety, while she waits.
There are the quaking leaves in the fall.

Where is she now, your Canadian girlfriend?
Leaf-taking has turned to winter,
the rains to crystal, and that love,
which was once an exhalation of flowers,
deeds you now the hardhack of the plains.
Some of the land is hilly here, and some flat;
and the heart, the same. And that is that.

JAMES BERTOLINO *was born near Hurley, Wisconsin, in 1942. He graduated in 1970 from the University of Wisconsin– Oshkosh, where he won a Book-of-the-Month Club poetry prize in his senior year. After studying a year at Washington State University, he went to Cornell University where he received an M.F.A. in 1973—joining the faculty the following year; he is currently teaching at the University of Cincinnati. A winner of the "Discovery '72" competition at the Poetry Center, New York City, he has published frequently in periodicals. His most recent volume of poems is* Employed *(Ithaca House).*

THE RED DRESS

The whirr
of the sewing machine

her back
  bent
beautiful in the tension
of her toil

the purr
of my thread
   between
her fingers

brings her to me,
brings us,
weaves me in the house
of her

& nowhere
is there stronger
more soft
  fabric
than this

EVE OF JULY FOURTH

A hound twitches
with the sound
of vomit
as a party breaks up

Two people make it
without love
on dry, desperate ground

Alone
a child weeps
as bats whisper past
her damp pillow

In the red buzz
of an emergency flare
an old man punishes
furiously
a mosquito
        his sun-tanned

grandson
hunts nightcrawlers
on his knees
in the dark
        eyes aglint

with silver-
speckled fish

& fireworks

EMPLOYED

I quit my job this morning.

They couldn't understand
ducks
rippling across my mind
from shore to weeds & back
or down for grub.

What's more I didn't care
for their caring to keep me
behind a counter. Blue

moving into green on the hills
& the black snake
with red stripes the length of its body

stretch my eyes
beyond books

tell me I'm right,
I'm right.

JAMES BERTOLINO / 25

BEYOND THE STORM

The storm has come again today,
it rages shrill pins.
I hear a pale child
moaning alone
by the bottom rocks of the field.
I feel the blowing wet
bruise her face.

Three days have been
since Marlys left
in her wool coat, winding
down the fright of the path, dark.
The branches are knives.
Out of lulling wind comes quacking,
a duck on the raft.

I can't remember how long
the fire's been cooled,
& my legs are twitching more today.
Stomach too moans more than hunger;
I'm afraid.

Lying here the shadows make shapes
with my hand. The storm
is subsiding. There's a cricket
under the bed.

THE MARRIAGE

I am a turtle
with a lead shell,
with fragile blue wings
of gossamer
& small.
The sky is far
when you say you're through.

You are a bobcat
with thin claws of glass,
with grey dreamy eyes
of no luster.
The green tall trees
are emery
when I say I don't love you.

Night comes.
The air is sparse,
the ground cold.
Our eyes round owls
afraid in the dark.
Give me your hand,
it will hold us.

JAMES BONK *was born in Chicago, Illinois, in 1932. His poems have appeared in* Choice, Commonweal, America, Minnesota Review, Yankee, *and a number of other publications. Bonk earns his living as a health association executive, and he, his wife, and his three sons live in Mount Prospect, Illinois.*

ELEGY FOR A POLISH GRANDAUNT

Chicago
In the lisping drizzle,
bell-tower
of St. Adalbert church
tongue   tongue
2 old men
pull ropes
tongue   tongue
to tell
this dying Polish island
of 18th Street
about your requiem.

We,
the better-off relations
come down here now
only to bury,
and that briskly;

Yet,
no one hurries a Black Mass,
or the wonderful, hypocritical,
solemnity of the slow walk
behind the cross & the copes
to the 6 tall candles in front

where the old Adalbert,
mitered, white and widearmed,

stands on the tabernacle
like a frozen sea god
ruling a sunken temple
of grey, slavic onyx.

Office of the Dead:
    black marble streaked
    with white hopes.

Forced to forget nothing,
we sang the farewell hymn
at the church doors, and at
the cemetery out on Milwaukee Ave.
1 by 1 threw wilted petals
like tired prayers
over your casket.

All my life
I wanted a word
    for your gestures,
    for the mystery
    of your deliberate symbols,
    for the strangeness
    of Christmases
    at your house
    and my child ear
    cut off by English.

The word,
I think now,
was dignity;
and somehow
we buried you
with it.

If you ever wondered
    while you waited
    at Oak Forest

like a bird
of dry brown leaves,
eyes filming,
you needn't have.
No Alderman,
no local judge
now downtown,
was ever buried better.

ACROPHOBE & LAPIDARY

When I was a visiting nephew of 10,
an ancient uncle of my mother took me
outside of Ottawa where the sand mines died
and the grey hills of hardened silica sparked
in their studdings of Fool's Gold. Silent and seamed
as the indian on my cigar box, old
stooped uncle stood dreaming while I mucked for stars
in the clay bottoms of the blood-red iron
pools. By dark, my box bulged with chunks of glitter.

Since then, I have sat in the hollow circles
of the seers, and on lucid nights have heard sounds
above their incantations: Hopkins hanging
on his cliffs of fall, and Rimbaud, ears ringing,
beating at the gates of God. For what? There's no
life at those heights though the doors be hammered gold.
I would rather chip the sharp mud from my dross
in the dark, where the drop is only to the floor.

PAINTING AN OLD APARTMENT

Symphonie Fantastique

Midnight on my ladders, FM blasting, and three beers
have me in tune with Berlioz. Trumpets and drums march
his half-dead poet to the gallows, while on my own
jigging scaffold, I celebrate the Witches' Sabbath
with tuba groans of *Dies Irae*, and look for love
themes in the faded wallpaper. I could be as bored
as old Michelangelo crawling the catwalks
of the Sistine ceiling; but instead, I feed
the lean peacock of humility by performing
this knowing, futile act: laying my layer
on the deepening strata of melancholy dwellers here.
And my art must be as secret as the woodworker
who carved these grotesque circles over the doorposts.
Tonight, I know the pain of his slow, forgotten efforts;
his craft was in the cutting—mine in the covering.
Together, our work will wait the new discoverers.

WALTER BRADFORD, *born in Chicago, Illinois, in 1937, is a founding member of the Organization of Black American Culture (OBAC). He has held the Gwendolyn Brooks Writing/Traveling Fellowship, and has published in* Nommo, Black World, Black Expressions, Journal of Black Poetry, Panorama *(Chicago Daily News), and the anthology* Jump Bad. *Bradford has taught at Malcolm X College and Roosevelt University, and presently teaches creative writing at the Womens' Division of Cook County Jail for the Northeastern University Center for Inner City Studies (Chicago).*

T.C.

(Terry Callier; True Christian)

And the voices dropped
                    from the ashy ceiling like pellets of rain
foreshadowing his coming;
            "A Gemini's Sun" they cried, "born to trudge
between the parallels of the heavenly twins."
            And he does that with a guitar for a crucifix and six thin
palms for strings (all of them mean actors)
                            while strolling down the dan
ry-an eXpressway, with a forty pound VOO DOO radiator
        on his back and
a red ban-dan-na tied around his head singing, "I have seen
        all the light!"
            While some stillborn monkey niggahs
                            with steel knuckles for asses
in chartreuse pants and fishtail shoes, swing ape-style on the
        51st
street overpass screaming: "Moses, is you back again?"
And they streamed on behind him till the concreteness
            stopped at
the base of MECCA'S hill
                            just to hear
                            TERRY CALLIER SING!
        And young 63rd street pharaohs cloaked in Blackstone's
            label gave

peace hosannas to Disciples, for
                          creation was order, it was peace.
    So instead of some bible-fiction god rebuilding this world
      let
Nommo-child Terry Callier sing the first seven days.
    True christian, please make your world.

A POEM FOR FOSTER

> *Life under natural conditions is*
> *"nasty, brutish and short."*
> HOBBS

Once when you were a star
and shining was all you knew
you sped around clusters and egos
on your way to god
and gave yourself the proceeds of love
the work you called your own.
Then, from where winds come
a rush of life calling you home;
talking is a thing you do, living is what you are.
Brother, you taught this—a reason in the wind—
long songs of holy life pasted on a page;
you knew it, had made it, how did it
get you down?
Now, you are dead
a slit inside the earth
a line on a stone
a virtue passed.
But I know
what you feel at night
alone-you and it-alone
pop-daddy
the scag hero from the East
has got you
has got you
down.

A POEM WITH A CONCLUSION

It wasn't always this way for us
us had times before that were good as any
like what you said when I came home bent, and slightly
unproud, "I won't yo' big head rite here!"
And how in those fly times
us burned love clean through
so fierce and perfected,
the world was blessed by us.
And when us made screams and grunts of help
in the middle of the night (and daytime too)
but us really didn't need any
and how us shined the window
so tomorrow had uh 'hole to come through
and one us could look out
and see what it would bring . . .
us had it all
sweet mama
fine, sweet city mama
us had it all . . .
But now
we have
said good-bye
have said good-bye
with out
the words.

FRANKLIN BRAINARD, *born in 1920, has been a teacher and, most recently, poet-in-residence for the Mounds View, Minnesota, public schools. His latest volume was published by the Minnesota Writers' Publishing House in 1973, and his poems have appeared in* Epos, Perspective, Café Solo, *and many other magazines. He lives in New Brighton, Minnesota.*

ROUBAIX CEMETERY

I have looked at the Roubaix Cemetery:
its pines have fallen from another world,
have caught a mountainside
to hold the rupture and the carving of an age
while eating it slowly.

When sun comes the earth is speckled
like the breast of a grouse,
the columns of created light
carrying dust older and finer than soil.

I have looked into the Roubaix Cemetery
where bones of the Finlanders lie
undertaker straight,
boxed against the raw half soil
and rawer stones.

Their passions are somewhere else
dancing;
their old hands that grew to tools
no longer milk,
no longer turn the separator;
their madness no longer asks them, "Why?"

Let me lie there.
I shall leave the troubles of my marrow,
shall leave my madness,
shall leave the loves I've ruptured,

and, in the grouse light,
climb the columns of dust
and disappear in sun.

RAINGATHERER

I have said, "Dear God," under my breath a thousand times.
Rolling I have wrapped the thousand night sheets around the
    days
I could not reach, could not hold.
Each day is just beyond my fingers:
my madness, my family's madness, the world's.
Our Father have mercy on us who gather rain.
Our Father have mercy on me
one of these the least of Your raingatherers.
In a world of earthenware I come with a paper cup.

INLAND SEA

Here in the wind-shave of prairie land
through senses the animal did not think about
I feel the swell of seas
and in my mouth
waking
I taste salt.
My tiredness rises to a breaking.
I shall be coral for an unknown reef
of grass.
I shall be lime to green.
I shall yellow cactus flowers.
Because I live
because I love this living
because this animal would die to live
I'll die to rise again
as seasonal.
I shall be salt for absent Agassiz
lifting now to grass.

WHITE ROPES

Yesterday's December rain
turned snow this morning
The wind brought white ropes to hold us
and the cattle and horses turned
in their ancient ritual
to head downwind.
I could have read this
if I wished
as the freezing of life
but this isn't so.
The ranch dog, sheep-white with snow,
will not come in;
his life is outside.
There is an endurance,
with hope,
as perennial and seasonal as grass.
The cattle and horses
paw the snow and browse,
and the dog comes to meet me.
I wonder about my place
in the metaphor,
assume mine is theirs.
I turn in,
thinking of the white storm
in my blood:
leukemia;
turn in
remember horses,
remember cattle,
remember dog,
remember badland cedars
knotting up to sun
in land so dry
no tree should grow.
I turn out again
and you
may have the harvest
of my marrow.   FRANKLIN BRAINARD / 37

GEORGE CHAMBERS, *born in Cambridge, Massachusetts, in 1931, teaches at Bradley University in Peoria, Illinois. He has had recent work in* Kamadhenu, TriQuarterly, *and* Ark River Review. *In 1974, an interview and a selection of poems were published in the* Voyages to the Inland Sea *series (University of Wisconsin–La Crosse).*

THE VOICE

I can tell you. Thin ditches
cut along tar roads in my
country. I watch ice form
on greasy weeds. I hear a
tin cup tapping on a pump
outside my door. In the morning
I boil an egg and sit in the kitchen.
I drink black coffee, read the label
of a peanut butter jar. I know it
by heart. This morning I followed
strawberries on the tablecloth
with my finger. I can tell you this.

THE LIFE

I live with the mad woman
on a bluff behind the sun.
The roads are iced for hours
at a time. The beer ran out
yesterday. She has a pretty
limp, she loves the universal
vegetable. For pleasure
I draw clean lines on paper
with my finger. I make
rectangles and fill in

the holes with pretty
names of people and also
their pretty faces.
The mad woman says I am crazy
to beat her on Saturday
and call the sun such bad
names, such altogether
bad names. She says she
will pack her names and
leave me with my finger
unless I kiss the cat
she thinks she has.
The mad woman says I must
be mad to sit on the bluff
to put everything I see
in holes and not tell her.
But I cannot tell
what will be right to do
or even what it might
make sense to say.
Lately the mad woman and I
have been talking about
the sea, wondering if we
can make room for her
here behind the bluff.
And lately she is singing
the joy of shoes and
telling me if I feed her
she will love me. Tomorrow
we plant our beans in
the windy field. She will say
it's a silly thing to do.

D. CLINTON, *born in 1946, is completing work toward his M.F.A. in poetry at Bowling Green State University. He has participated in Poetry in the Schools projects in Kansas, Ohio, and Montana. Clinton has published poems in* Falcon, The Little Magazine, Mikrokosmos, Midwest Quarterly, Kansas Quarterly, *and* Poetry Now.

BREATHING, AT LAST, IN THE WICHITA ART MUSEUM

The shroud keeps scratching my eyes my nuts my
Cranium splits on impact from the skinny pick.
Chemicals dazzle me. Sand pours into my
Sockets. The special crane they've got
Looks technical. The display case gives off
Odd reflections. Unwrapped. The Sunday lookers
Appear horrified.
For Britain and novelty's sake, the Rockefeller
Family passes me through customs and the Atlantic
For a Talking Midwest Guggenheim Tour, talking
To kids on shrouds, sand and the *real* source
Of the Nile in small lecture halls in
Hays, Garnett, Emporia, Fredonia,
Eureka, Winfield and Pittsburg. Before I know it,
The Permanent Gifts Room hoists me out
Of the Mobile Arts Truck for measurement
Through the basement of the Wichita Art Museum.
They case me up neat, like a *coup d'état*, with a white
4 x 5 card, next to Goya, next to macramé: a good
Spot after 25 lazy centuries.

VICTOR CONTOSKI *was born in Minneapolis, Minnesota, in 1936. His work has appeared in* Quixote, Kayak, Chicago Review, Hearse, *and several other "little magazines."* Broken Treaties, *his most recent book, was published by New Rivers Press in 1973. He lives in Lawrence, Kansas, and teaches American literature and various poetry courses at the University of Kansas.*

THE KANSA

1

The Kansa, wind people,
south wind people,
told their children The Beginning.

The first man and woman
grew from earth on an island.
Water everywhere.
Many children came,
quarrelled with their parents
and made children of their own
with no place to put them.

Then animals sprung from the earth
the small ones, friends,
beavers, muskrats, turtles,
who dived into the water,
brought up mud
and built, earth on earth,
and the island grew.

2

Then trees poked out,
put forth leaves
that flew and became birds.

Grass grew on the land.
Deer came and buffalo
to be food and clothes for the Kansa.

3

And ever the land increased,
grew rough, heaved, divided;
and man also divided.

Earth People
the first to pitch tents
who knew the season for moving
knew the season for waiting.

Thunder People
who soothed storms
by casting cedar leaves
into the campfire
and burned prairie grass
to bring rain.

Buffalo People
sacred to the shaggy beast
sought him in the hunt
and could not eat his flesh
until others had done.

Ghost People
the first eaters at funerals
who took horses as payment
from relatives of the new dead.

Each to his element,
each in his season.

4

And after many winters
the buffalo moved to new

pastures onto the plains
leading the wind people westward
to the land of their name
the flat land that
remembered its past
that remembered water.

5

And the Kansa moved out
to the Great Plains of the Midwest
carrying their medicines,
their pipes and holy sea shells
to the Kaw River Valley.

There they lived
till white men found them:
Fool Chief by Big Soldier Creek
Hard Chief by Red Vermillion Creek
American Chief by Mission Creek
White Plume by the Wakarusa.

There they waited with the buffalo
to be pushed south
toward the wind
of their name
toward extinction.

PETER COOLEY, *born in Detroit, Michigan, in* 1940, *teaches in the College of Creative Communication at University of Wisconsin–Green Bay. His poems have appeared in* American Review, The New Yorker, Partisan Review, Harper's, *and in the anthology* New Voices in American Poetry. *He is poetry editor for* North American Review.

TRACKS

Midnight. The words start out, walking
from the poem I've been writing.
It snows. They go like snowflakes
to some point of silence
beyond this window, ridges of the road,
snow's been piling all day.

Now they're running, their boots
like the thunder of nails
building a house. It snows.
Their faces are hard & sheer
ice bent into this.
          So hard
I can't tell if you're still here
(it snows) since I've started to say it:
everywhere we are is snow.
The page is coming toward you, quickly
under a noon sun. It could melt.

PACKER CITY POEM

Nothing is getting up now in my life
like lawns of the neighbors at evening
shaved flanks bared to the stars,
the factories' tentacles of smoke.

If I watered you, could you develop,
I ask Ennui, putting it to her
limply. Even her boobies are bored,
padded, cold. Help, help, I'm up the middle
of middle america & can't break out
a cheer announces from my throat.
Linemen flake the t.v.'s grin
like autumn leaves; wiser, birds V
in mid-July for winter camp & beer
freezing here in June. And now a lady
pares her next door hedge with frost
on nails & stacked-up hair. Dogsleds,
a snowmobile, one of your miracles, quick,
angel. Summer, I winter here,
I diet on rich air. Another year?

THE REVENANT

There is a light in the snow
which stretches, edgeless like a desert
on the window, *pure mirage*
I'd say except I've seen it
rise, at the end of a field
while I froze there, wrapped & bright
in that terror I've shown for an angel
putting clear bones flush to the wind.

Then it will shake like a half-moon
blossom on a tropical plant,
above the horizon, between trees,
ruts in the road, the stubble
where she straightens herself, ready
before me on both white thighs
which start walking slowly, very slowly, into me.

When it is over I shake myself out
of the skin of it, saying to myself
you have slept in blood & sapphires once
again; but sage nor magus never knew it,
for this is clearer than water & before it
yet the shape is holy, mine like a dream
by which a man might float
in the necessary dark, a candle,
a needle we long to pass through
with ease, as if the whole world
in that moment which stands still
were being called home.

DAVID CURRY *was born in Springfield, Illinois, in 1942. He still lives in Illinois' capital city, where he publishes the poetry magazine* Apple. *He is the author of* Here *(New Rivers Press, 1970) and* Theatre *(The Best Cellar Press, 1973.)*

THINKING BACK SEVEN YEARS
AND BEING HERE NOW

Thumbing through someone else's book
in a sublet New York apartment,
I found intense marginal notes
written in a curious backhand.

None of them made sense to me.
Passages in the text were underlined,
and I couldn't imagine why.
Bold exclamation points
drew me to words that did not astound.

The book and the notes were written
in the language I was born to
by men with flesh like mine.

Outside my window was the world.

Ahead of me was the future I have come to.
While you do what you do wherever you are,
I shall walk to the Midway Liquor Store
("the largest in Central Illinois")
under a Springfield winter's grey-white sky
and cherish it.

I AM OF THESE

My mother's fingers that have decorated cakes,
threaded needles and defeated cowlicks
are bent now. Still they make

a gold lyre among flowers
on a field of wine, a cover
for my father's organ bench.

"You're a very clever dame,"
my father says, taking his place
on this new thing she has made for him.
It is a line repeated throughout their lives,
familiar as a good tune.

He plays "Stardust" for her,
and she smiles, watching him rock
to reach the pedals. When she goes
to the kitchen, he switches to Dixieland.

"Not so damned loud!" she shouts,
and he makes it louder to drown her out.
She expects that. It is an antagonism
that love accommodates. They are each other's
worn, rehearsed, and undiminished joys.

PHILIP DACEY *was born in Saint Louis, Missouri, in 1939, and was educated at Saint Louis University, Stanford University, and the University of Iowa. His poems have appeared in* Esquire, Poetry, Poetry Northwest, Denver Quarterly, Massachusetts Review, North American Review, *and many other publications. At the present time he is coordinator of the creative writing program at Southwest Minnesota State College and editor of the poetry journal* Crazy Horse.

LOOKING AT MODELS IN THE SEARS CATALOGUE

These are our immortals.
They stand around
and always look happy.
Some must do work,
they are dressed for it,
but stay meticulously
clean. Others
play forever,
at the beach, in backyards,
but never move
strenuously. Here
the light is such
there are no shadows.
If anyone gestures,
it is with an open
hand. And the smiles
that bloom everywhere
are permanent, always
in fashion.
       So
it is surprising to discover
children here,
who must have sprung
from the dark of some loins.
For the mild bodies

of these men and women
have learned to stay
dry and cool:
even the undressed
in bras and briefs
could be saying,
It was a wonderful dinner,
thank you so much.
                    Yet,
season after season,
we shop here:
in Spring's pages,
no ripe abundance
overwhelms us;
in Winter's pages,
nothing is dying.
It is a kind of perfection.
We are not a people
who abide ugliness.
All the folds in the clothing
are neat folds,
nowhere to get lost.

THE ANIMALS' CHRISTMAS

They are always living
in Christmas.
Though they walk years
through a field
they can never step

out of the birth of a god.
In each dark brain
a star
sending light through their sinews
leads their hooves

forward from one miracle
to another,
the gleams
tipping grass
like the bright eyes

of uncountable millions
of babies
a field has borne.
When they rub a tree,
a secret myrrh

descends onto their backs.
They carry and offer it
without even trying.
From their nostrils
they breathe good news.

ANNIVERSARY

Five years.
The wooden anniversary.
We like wood, believe it's
trustworthy.

You have this thing for trees.
Phallic, maybe, but
I've seen gnarled, branching trees
light your eyes.

And wooden sculpture,
for us, has roots,
is still wet
with under-earth.

Our house will be wood.
We'll grow into it
like living wood ourselves,
branching out with children,

and it will grow
into us, turning us
supple but strong
in storms.

I say this: each anniversary
of our wedding
will amaze us
with its rich smell of wood.

ROBERT DANA, *born in 1929, has taught at Cornell College in Mount Vernon, Iowa, since 1954. His poetry has appeared in* The New Yorker, The Nation, Paris Review, *and elsewhere. His most recent work is* The Power of the Visible. *The poems included here are from a lengthy sequence entitled "Natural Odes/American Elegies."*

FROM "NATURAL ODES/AMERICAN ELEGIES"

38
We had known from the beginning this could happen

As we had known
that when the light is young
the river swift under its own unmoving silver
and the maples tasseled out with sun
two might marry in a look

As we had known
(one song ringing on all the radios of summer meaning mean-
    ing)
how feeling is the furthest edge of thought

Now I'm alone

Underfoot
frost sizzles in the long grass
Light pours from the wreck of the moon
Pressures of heaven I cannot read

And you are your own child
best and worst

Deafened with kisses
lamed by affection
whatever we had hoped for against time stretched like cold
    skin over the bones

against the shadow entering the blood like a calm fraction
was a road leading to

To distinguish love from use
'the only ideas are those of the shipwrecked'
some notion of wave and passing
a case of water   wind   fire
the grace of stones

No use asking why
Ask what we ever were to each other
that mattered

39
Christmas day
and the pines misted above the heavy snow

A bird ghosts the far clearing

All of this sleeps in the President's head

His radar whispers
and universities fall out of the sky
the rot of cities
the milk of poverty in your letters saying 'I love you'
and 'I still love you but goodbye'
fall toward their targets

When the black kiss explodes
and gut ribbons out in the unbelievable decompression
or the heart ruptures in those silver altitudes

it is not more
than the scream in the streets
when the gift of fire opens itself

How then shall the child be known
the carpenter bleeding into the beautiful grain of his labor
the mother her breasts blown away
How then shall the ash of the grandfathers be honored

As I walk the wheel-rutted snow
following my own tracks of the day before
and those of the dog and a man on bear-paws

I come to your name
where I knifed it into the snow
and I try to shape one word I can believe

42
It was not quite winter
when we first walked here

The blue air dripped and spattered
The flags of the lookout sweated cold

Damp limestone upon stone

Across the river
the trees had banked their wet fires
'God moves in the wind' you said 'if he moves at all'

Today
in this not quite spring

the wind full
the sun like silver birds
flocking the water with its passion

We hunker
against the south sides of stones

warm and animal

for Peg

A . A . D E W E Y , *born in* 1947, *is the assistant director of an experimental college at the University of Kansas; he also teaches courses in contemporary American literature and creative writing. His poems have appeared in* New York Quarterly, The Smith, Hanging Loose, Hearse, Café Solo, Cottonwood Review, *and other literary magazines.*

AT THE DRIVE-IN: "JOHN WAYNE VS. GOD"

The sound of faint thunder
was silenced by the volume
of his voice.

But black clouds rolled in;
lightning hit the power lines,
and John Wayne vanished.

God won,
and the red-necks
dumped the beer cans
and tore out in their
American-flagged pickups,
looking for some ass.

THE COYOTE

I saw it jerking as I drove by.
It was nailed by its tail
to the top of a fence post—left
hanging to die, already mauled
by the dogs that had caught it.

The eyes closed. The
head hung still. I
cocked my rifle.
It waited.

THE BLIZZARD

Cattle huddle together,
their butts sticking out
to keep from smothering
in the swirls . . .
just-born calves
and lost cows
the exception.

When it is done,
and snow has polished snow
with its rasping,
dark upturned legs
rise against that brilliance,
marking the place
for the crows.

R. P. DICKEY *was born in Flat River, Missouri, in* 1936, *and grew up in nearby Elvins (the "Lead River" of his fourth book,* Concise Dictionary of Lead River, Mo.). *He has taught at the University of Missouri and Southern Colorado State College. A textbook,* The Basic Stuff of Poetry, *was published by Kendall/ Hunt Publishing Co., Dubuque, Iowa.*

HUMIDITY

Went out to plant some tomatoes,
down to shoot a few goals,
went out to dig potatoes,
out for a little squirrel hunting,
and worked up a sweat,
ubiquitous chrism! a liquid
plague on all our houses
under the boiling midwest sun
or too many overcast skies,
summer, fall, winter, spring,
every other day it seems
this pervasive, sticky, gloggy,
uncolored gangrene of the body
of the breathing world or this
part of it S. O. Bewley once called
anus mundi when he said, "When
they want to take the temperature
of the world, they stick a rectal
thermometer in Lead River, Mo."

SHAZAM

When we'd make the rounds
every couple of weeks
to trade comic books,
we'd seldom stop at George Staley's house,
right on the edge of downtown,
behind Goggin's Drilling Company.
He never *had* many.

But one day he climbed
to the top of Mrs. Carver's shed
with a towel on his back
for a cape, hollered "Shazam"
so loud Charley Sebastian could hear,
and dove off into thin air. Actually
flew for a instant, then came
the crash, boom, bam that cracked
his collar bone and might have killed him
if he hadn't been so limber and fat.
George *kept* most of the comic books he had.

X

That's the way Tod Johnson signed
his name, after first rubbing his nose
and saying, Right here, huh? Right here.

That's where Ron Dickson and his two kids
in their station wagon got smashed by
a big Baltimore & Ohio that couldn't stop.

Where we had our treasure buried
in a metal chest—pearls, rubies, emeralds,
seven cents and a Mickey Mouse watch.

The fox-hole we dug back from the highway.
The car would stop, the guy reach over, we'd
pull the rope to jerk the suitcase and cut out!

Where Bear Phipps allegedly did on or about
the night of August 10, 1947, rape Pat McCutcheon,
being his first cousin according to law.

That's down behind Beck's restaurant
where with rocks and .22's we killed
over 33 water moccasins in one day.

The dead middle of town intersection
where we'd always stand to hitchhike,
heading for Flat River, St. Louis, Timbuktu.

Fred Fallen's chicken farm, from
where his mad son Ron would zoom
down on his Harley maybe standing on the seat.

Chris Weiss lived about there, blind
in one eye, chewing Beech-Nut, carving
pick handles, hammer handles, hoes and violins.

Wood's Drug Store was where everyone stood
around out front all dressed up wanting
to know "Where's everybody at?" all the time.

Across the street, City Hall. Once we crushed
some fig bars, shaped a turd—man, you should
have heard the Clerk holler when he found it!

The graveyard beside the Methodist Church.
Once Wanda Hughes didn't want to do it out there
so we sneaked inside on the carpeted aisle.

That's about where Jeri Wilson had her baby
on the Greyhound bus coming down from St. Louis.
Month early, no complications. A boy.

Where Jess Freeman woke up when they found
him out sleepwalking with his shorts on—
right in front of old lady Carver's house!

That's about where the shoe factory stood,
where Chris Weiss would never work, and
next to it a place where a guy kept ponies.

That's a chat dump, there's another one,
and another one right over there—
actually sand more than chat—and *there*.

Good rabbit hunting country all around
in through here, and ducks on these lakes;
once saw a deer right about—there.

That's the main drag, where people go
pigeon-toed, bowlegged, knockneed, pot-
gutted, limping, big-eyed, little footed,

in clothes hiding moles, scars, low
shoulders, warts, and corsets—
but some of them are pretty fine.

Right there's the place I grew up in.

STEPHEN DUNN *was born in New York City in 1939, educated at Hofstra and Syracuse universities, and presently teaches creative writing at Southwest Minnesota State College in Marshall, Minnesota. In addition to publishing widely in magazines, he has published one collection of poems,* Looking for Holes in the Ceiling *(University of Massachusetts Press, 1974), and a chapbook,* 5 Impersonations *(Ox Head Press, 1971). Dunn was a winner of the "Discovery '71" award from the Poetry Center, New York City.*

THE CITY BOY

Minnesota, 1973

He lives near a grain elevator, farms
on all sides. Everyone knows his name.
Amazing! The stars get through to the eye
at night. He hasn't been afraid for a year.

But wherever he goes, a foreigner goes with him.
He stands on the flat land, unsure
of his balance. He dreams of his silhouette
stuck against the sky.

From his warm house in an immaculate season
he begins the poem again, the one
in which the city, coughing now,
gone to pieces, is forgotten.

It hangs on. It hangs on.

GIRAFFES: THE AMERICAN VERSION

When the giraffes left their silos in Iowa
there were huge vacancies in the land.
Owners put ads in the papers, "Space Available."
Wheat came with its golden money,
rented them for a winter, had no complaints
and stayed on.

In Africa, to this day, the tops of trees
think they invented the giraffe out of
an evolutionary need to be loved. They know
nothing of the silos, nor the long voyage
across the sea in which several giraffes
became periscopes, masts, sea monsters.

Two or three giraffes, who had been educated
and consequently thought they were taller
than water, drowned. When they decomposed
bananafish built a temple among their bones.
To swim between their ribs was a sin. To sleep
in their skulls meant there'd be a perfect day
ahead. Plankton wandering in were sacrificed.

Giraffe worship remains rare but fervent.
Giraffes, for example, are the tribal animals
of the Neowhi, a band of savages near the heart
of darkness. They believe giraffes know
what the sky thinks, when the mountain will
spill into their lives. At Christmas time
they ask the giraffe statue if
they should murder, if the sun will come up.

Lately, giraffes who've been chosen for zoos
and who've heard their grandfathers talk about Iowa
come in high on nectarines to their physicals,
flunk them, and are sent back to the jungle.
There, by no accident, lions wait
with their terrific mouths, the size of cities.

THE CYCLE

Again,
smoke starts to rise from chimneys,
and out of the mouths of pastors.
It is almost winter. It is almost
Sunday every day of the week.
The elemental struggles begin, always,
as if they have never begun.
Someone makes a fire. A child dies,
or a wheatfield. Then a parent invents
hell. Then a farmer gives up sex.
And a young man comes forward, begins
to speak about why the darkness comes
so regularly, why the mysterious hands
beneath the soil have moods. The town
goes quiet. The air that surrounds him
is a thousand years old.
He is given gifts, and a beating.
He is sent away to school.
He returns. He is returning.
Women stock their pantries
with soup cans and crucifixes.
Children think ahead to Christmas,
the fat red Christ.
The fires go out. They are lit again.
The snow comes. The ancestors of
ancestors huddle in our bodies.
Their dreams rise to our heads.

FOR THE SLEEPLESS

1

It's late. Dark. A swatch of moonlight
on the floor. Outside, a streetlamp
spreading its solitude.
There's a frog sitting in the light it makes,
happy as a stone.
Here comes someone, always, always.
The frog leaps for darkness.
I try to hide behind the shade.

2

Two in the morning. The cacaphony
of asphalt and a kicked tin can.
I go to the window, my nakedness
with me like an angry friend.
A man seems to have found a tune
for his loneliness. I am tired
of good reasons. I hate him like a woman
hates a woman in identical clothes.

3

Awakened by the absolute silence
of snow, I imagine my feet
leaving a clear trail somewhere.
It is not yet dawn. I touch my nose,
which is cold: the dead, frozen bird
I stuffed in the garbage
appears before my eyes.

4

Dawn. I am perfectly still,
warm, conscious.
My mother, in a dream,
has just risen from the dead.
It was not disturbing.
A cock from a nearby farm reminds me
that, almost every day, things begin
without me.

THE DREAM

The edge of town disappears.
Then the fog lifts, I am covered
with wet grass, rent money
in my fist, and I can't remember
my name, which may be Blackie
but I'm not sure.
I check my knees
which are trying to leave me.
I call out to my toes which my wife
sometimes uses to rake leaves.
They're intact. But why are pigs
doing algebra in the mud?
Why are horses loping toward me,
with big slave eyes?
Are these hints?
I head for the center of town
where the postman must know me,
but he's in the street, marks
my forehead "Fragile" with a rubber stamp
and whispers "There are no boundaries"
in my ear. I catch two Jaycees
looking in their pants for something
to change their lives.
And behind a barn which is moving
slowly down the street, thirty-six
farm girls are going to town.
An old man, could it be my father?
rolls past me like sagebrush.
I do not move.
When I finally locate my name
in a phone book, it is so narrow and final
I am disgusted with it, and I rush out
into the confusion with alternatives.

HARLEY ELLIOTT, *born in Mitchell, South Dakota, in 1940, is currently a teacher and a houseboat builder in Salina, Kansas. His second book of poetry,* All Beautyfull & Foolish Souls, *was published by The Crossing Press, and three more books are scheduled to appear soon. Elliott is a frequent contributor to many of the best literary magazines.*

PASSING STOCKYARDS WHERE THEY KILLED THE BUFFALO

There's one in every city
stacked on the most distant
artery of commerce
like bloody shoes in the back
of a closet

and to each of them a buffalo
is somehow delivered and there shot dead
tightly knurled hump of hair
great bones and black nose
plowing into the soft
outskirts of town.

It is such nonsense
passing this in a strange city
my friend saying 'there's where
they shot the buffalo'
and my unguarded face
opens into tears.

Not for manhandled nobility
or the buffalo's steaming heart
but that we stand still
in the sudden light of the moment
while butchers cross the sunset
in their yellow rubber gowns.

Rainy skulls rise in the country
skeletons in creekbeds
all secrets yet to be
broken from the fields

and the violet November dusk
curves over us. Those we love
are finishing a glass of milk
or turning from a doorway
disappearing in the distant
borders of the sky.

CHANGING A TIRE BY THE MISSOURI RIVER

Turning the nuts one at a time
at midnight on a country road
the cold clear black air
pours into my body

and a mile away the invisible
Missouri River slides along.
You stand in the headlights' yellow
corridors of light

wrapped in a blanket
impenetrable fields on either side
where farm dogs call and
the distant coyotes answer.

We have one child asleep
in the car   another turning
with stars in your body.
On the giant billboard a dreamy

cowboy is lifting a slice
of bacon to his mouth.
I see my hands glow

with the lovely moment
of changing this tire.

The four way wrench slowly revolves.
I am entering my life.

BEFORE THE FROST

Tonight I am one of a number
of men in mackinaws
getting to their gardens

just before the frost
bringing in the phantom watermelons
late cucumbers

and baskets of blue
and purple tomatoes
under the october moon

the night is so clear
we can read our thoughts
in each rising breath

and all the way across
to colorado I feel the dark
poised groups of deer

a russet colored bear
crawling down the mountain rim.

THE RESIDENT STRANGER

There is your brain
floating map of your life
a dreaming grey cauliflower
surrounded by clouds.

There is the room
filled with future voices—
the voice of your death
the voice of your absence
the voice of your birth
they flow together like layers of a river.

And here is a vault of wishes and fears
a prayer for your cells.
Your body appears
in all its disguises
the 98 lb weakling
the beefcake hero   the laughing
hyena of madness
and the masks of disease
lie waiting in the corner.

This room holds only knowledge.
An attic of mementos
highway signs and textbook pages.
All you ever knew
of letters and numbers
rising in cold steam
behind sealed windows.

Secrets fill the
keyhole of this door.
Your private fantasies stand around
like bus station vagrants.
Rape and murder are looking
for an exit
unaware of the trap
door in the floor.

Inside the last room
the resident stranger stands
his face a swirl
of dreams and memory
a procession of animals and
men looking at your life.

Along his thighs
languid butterflies open and close.
Your history is sung
by the wings of his back
one hand holds a stone
the other a plant.
When you love he flashes
across your face
at death he stands
radiant in the sockets of your skull.

OUTSIDE ABILENE

the full rage of kansas
turns loose upon us.

On the mexican radio station
they are singing *Espiritu de mis sueños*
and that is
exactly it tonight.

The spirit of my dreams
rises in the storm like vapor.

Deep clouds bulge together
and below them
we are a tiny constellation of lights
the car
laid under sheets of lightning
moving straight in to the night.

Before us are miles
and miles of water and wind.

DAVID ALLAN EVANS *was born in Sioux City, Iowa, in 1940. He has degrees from Morningside College and the University of Iowa, and he currently teaches creative writing, poetry, and composition courses at South Dakota State University in Brookings. His poems have appeared in numerous publications, including* Best Poems of 1969, Esquire, *the* New York Times, *and* North American Review. *He edited* New Voices in American Poetry *for Winthrop Publishers.*

THE CITIZENS' COMPLAINT

Sioux City, 1972

on their highest bluff
War Eagle's tomb
is eroding
knuckle by knuckle

into the Missouri

so they complain
call it unsightly

now there is talk
of the skull
visible all spring
impervious
even to flash floods

how do they explain
this thing?—

this enemy among them
gazing down on the city
with eyes full of rain
who will not fall

into the river

NEIGHBORS

They live alone
together,

she with her wide hind
and bird face,
he with his hung belly
and crewcut.

They never talk
but keep busy.

Today they are
washing windows
(each window together)
she on the inside
he on the outside.
He squirts Windex
at her face;
she squirts Windex
at his face.

Now they are waving
to each other
with rags,

not smiling.

SOME LINES AFTER THE RAZING OF THE SIOUX CITY ARMOUR'S PLANT

it is 5 A.M. everything is the same as it was
the moon-hammered faces of the cattle are waiting
the line at the hiring gate is growing minute by minute
you can see the faces of yesterday or last year
or forty years ago looking more eager than they are
the same hands hiding out in the same pockets
if you wait long enough the gate will open up
inside everything will be the same as it always was
you will see knives glittering like the Missouri
pulleys ribs barrels guts tanks bones chopping blocks
any tooth could tell you the same old story
any hide if you had time to listen

DOUG FLAHERTY, *born in* 1939, *teaches the poetry work-shop at the University of Wisconsin–Oshkosh. His work has ap-peared in* The Nation, The New Yorker, Poetry Northwest, Quarterly Review of Literature, *and other magazines. Recent chapbooks of his poetry include* Weaving a Slow Dream of Hands, Moving All Ways at Once, *and* Fleshed Out.

THE LAKE FLIES OF WINNEBAGO

swarm off the cool water
love up against the sun-
side of houses far inland
I think of the abbot Kwaisen
and his monks by free will
burnt alive by mad soldiers

So that even when Yen-t'ou
screamed as the skin bubbled
lungs filled with white
smoke of his own flesh
his scream was heard in
the distant folds of mountain

My mouth clogs with flies
as it opens surprised to tell you
the marauder lake flies have
come to test our will
descend upon us clothed
in spirit wings of old monks

Even later safe indoors
a cup poured for us both
the flowered sheets turned down
they whine and nudge
so deep the window
is dark by noon

RASPBERRIES

The fathers told us
how sparrows
ate a fill of berries
beat wings dropped
seeds across river
and years of growing
parted by waters
grew into flaming briar

If we believe
what the fathers say
about seeds cleansed
in dark stomachs
and if we start out
heading due north
knifing our bodies
against the current
we will fill a bucket
by last light of today

If we believe
in the guts of words
roots contained in seed
then we will know
that the sparrow
is a bullet
in the heart
of the living dead

COMING ON TO WINTER

for Tom McKeown

1

Snow falls like wedding rice,
taps my shoulder for a handout.
'It's your heart we're after.'

Below this field of sleeping seed,
shivering black rats clean
their nails for the feast.

2

So cold tonight I'm already asleep:
my mind trudges the arctic ocean floor,
my body space-walks the zodiac.

I break the spell, enter my house,
find the full-moon on my pillow.
Make room for an old lover.

3

Snow doesn't stop at the border.
Birds left before the air froze
a ceiling of ice over the fish's haunt.

I walk bear tracks over snow,
all night chanting to the stars.
Suddenly, I notice the prints fit.

ROBERT FLANAGAN *was born in Toledo, Ohio, in 1941. He served in the U.S. Marine Corps, received a B.A. at the University of Toledo, and earned his M.A. at the University of Chicago. He has taught writing courses in Chicago and Pennsylvania, and at present is an associate professor of English at Ohio Wesleyan University in Delaware, Ohio. His works include five poetry pamphlets published in the United States, Canada, England, and Northern Ireland; a book of poems,* The Full Round; *and a novel,* Maggot.

STATE MESSAGE: A MIDWESTERN SMALL TOWN

The dozen clocks of this courthouse
reflect a dozen different times.
A thirteenth is heard—erratic
ringing of tower chimes.

(Place is the only certain
fact we can live by:
the land may sprout a people,
a thing change to an I—

but it will not happen in time.
The wind does not root seeds.
A buried, measureless dream
is what growth needs.)

Above each clock I would place
a box to sound a voice:
This is chaos, or local clarity—
Citizen, it's your choice.

HEIRLOOM

The caprice of the strokes
caught here in time's hardening as a stray
bristle visible just beneath the gloss
like a single hair of an ice-locked mammoth—
a sooty, chipped blue,
a yellowed white beneath it streaked in cracks
weakly as a senile grin—
whoever tried to brighten this monstrous chest
a second time knew failure, stashed it
in the basement of the old house, is forgotten.

We take it in as ours,
stripping and sanding away paint
layers, blue, white, and surprise
into walnut, the strong dark grain
revived beneath the pressured circling
of our hands, like the ghostly image
of a greatgrandfather,
put underground long before our birth,
represented in a retouched tintype
centered in the reclining circle of his family
at what seems an outing, dancing
on the old sod what seems a hornpipe;
or one of him seated white-collared in dignity,
mustache waxed heavily as the walnut
breakfront behind him a dull gleaming.

Our hands complete their circles, though
we are full of aches. This dulling work
is redeemed by the use, more than worth,
of the chest. Restored, it will hold
what we in innocence call our own.

ATLAS

Lost in Oregon, hunting my bearings,
I open the road atlas, turning
accidently as a birthplace to Ohio,
Toledo inset in the upper corner,
to discover again, Detroit
and Monroe, the main thoroughfares
red Xed like cross hairs
over the city's heart,

and I sight as if through a scope
down years, past miles, to that point
in a boy's four-cornered world
where a railway apartment was
escape and prison. Summer heat
held nights by a flat tar roof
bore him to the living room floor.
On a mattress pad beneath open windows,

he watched in the dark until sleep
fabulous long-haul tractor-trailers
lit like beacons in the empty streets,
idling hugely, vibrant, at corners
waiting for the green to bear away
their burden of goods, going into
on eighteen singing eight-ply tires
an imaginable expanse of headlighted dark

twenty years past. Here,
studying the map of a city
as lost to me as Atlantis, I see
for the first recognizable time
beyond the hometown's Corporate
Limits, the crux of my youth,
those crossroads opening out,
becoming Interstate Routes.

DAN GERBER, *born in 1940, is also a novelist and journalist, and has taught at Thomas Jefferson College and at Michigan State University. He writes for* Sports Illustrated, *and his poems have appeared in* The New Yorker, The Nation, Stony Brook, Partisan Review, Ohio Review, Sumac, Hearse, *and others. Gerber has published two volumes of poems,* The Revenant *and* Departure *(Sumac Press), and two novels,* American Atlas *and* Out of Control *(Prentice-Hall). He lives near Fremont, Michigan.*

HOMECOMING

You return home
to find your house no longer there
The trees have grown back
and the toe of a boot you received for Christmas
protrudes through the loam of your floor
The door you locked in the morning
is the space between twilight
and the serialized stars
and your wife and children
their wings extended
circle the treetops
and sing indifferently of what you were

THE LINE

A day worth losing
flows by with the river

The brown skin of my hand
turns over a line
gathers slack from the current
lures dance
with the bones of my wrist

Each day there are messages
we ignore by the stream

The line moves
as stars flow
in patterns we judge a life by

No song but in my ear
a complexity of lives
lead   fire   rain
tar and couch grass
the picture in a million grey dots

The lines in my hand
flow off the edge
rivers of the world
irretrievably lost

        discipline discipline
channeling my life
in the music of the world

I have opened this line
to the threads of a milkpod
spunk smell of loam
effulgence of the brain
the idle lust of my eyes

THE TRAGEDY OF ACTION

Tomorrow afternoon
we will carry these books to the basement
tomorrow afternoon we will burn the tree
we will devise new ways
to protect us from our friends
and a list of everything
about which it is forbidden to worry

I have opened the window
The cold wind drives us to sleep
Tomorrow we will face a continuing life
consider grief a practical reality
death a robber of pleasure
this bed a preview
the fate of our children
the last bath   the last meal   the last click

Tomorrow
we will have forgotten
afraid something we might have said
would make a difference

GARY GILDNER, *born in 1938, is originally from Michigan,*
but he has lived in Des Moines, Iowa, since 1966. Three collections of
his poetry have been published by the University of Pittsburgh Press:
First Practice (1969), Digging for Indians (1971), *and* Nails
(1975). *He teaches at Drake University.*

TOURING THE HAWKEYE STATE

I saw the best parts of Iowa covered with New Jersey tea,
   partridge pea, rattlesnake master, and Culver's root,
   I saw Chief Keokuk's "X" in the county courthouse in
      Keokuk,
   home of John L. Lewis and Elsa Maxwell

I saw sweet William, wild rye, I saw the Iowa Watershed
      Divide
   running through the business district of Orient,
   I saw the outskirts of Adair and the locomotive wheel
   marking the spot where Jesse James derailed the Chicago,
   Rock Island and Pacific and knocked off engineer Rafferty
   and ran with the loot to Missouri

I saw gayfeather, blazing star, and butterfly weed,
   I saw where Henry Lott murdered Two Fingers on the
      banks
   of Bloody Run, where Dr. William S. Pitts, a dentist,
   wrote hymns, taught singing and practiced
   in Nashua in Chickasaw County,
   home of The Little Brown Church in the Vale,
   I saw Osage, home of Hamlin Garland.

I saw the home of Iowa's only one-eyed governor,
      Bill Larrabee,
   and Clarinda, home of Glenn Miller,
   and Humboldt, home of Frank Gotch, who hammerlocked
   the Russian Lion Hackenschmidt for the world

wrestling championship, and Grundy Center,
home of Herbert Quick, author of *The Hawkeye*,
The Invisible Woman, and others

I saw the braided rugs that Grant Wood's mother made
from Grant's old jeans, where the *Bertrand* went down
on her maiden voyage, taking boxes of Dr. Hostetter's
Celebrated Stomach Bitters, and the Fairview Cemetery
where Amelia Jenks Bloomer, of *The Lily*, lies buried,
I saw her Turkish pantaloons

I saw the only Holstein museum in America
and Mama Ormsby Burke's neck chain and milk stool
and the west branch of the Wapsinonoc and the modest
two-room cottage that sheltered young Herbert Hoover
and Peru where the first Delicious apple tree grew
and Newton, home of Emerson Hough, author of
    Mississippi Bubble

I saw the summit of Floyd's Bluff and the lightning-
struck obelisk south of Sioux City
near Interstate 29, the final resting place
of the bones of Sergeant Charles Floyd
who died of a busted gut under Lewis and Clark,
their only loss on the whole trip,
I saw Oskaloosa where Frederic K. Logan
composed "Over the Hills" and "Missouri Waltz"

I saw the Walnut, Turkey, Pony, Plum, and Honey creeks,
the Polecat River, Spirit Lake, the park where John Brown
drilled for Harper's Ferry, Eisenhower's Mamie's
home in Boone, the home of John "Duke" Wayne, né
    Marion M.
Morrision, in Winterset, Billy Sunday's mother's grave
a peg from Story County's Sewage Plant,
where Billy saw the light, where he came back
to gather souls, in Garner, after shagging flies in center
for the Chicago White Stockings

I saw ½ mile west of Orient where Henry Agard Wallace,
    experimentalist and Republican, Democrat and Progressive,
    breeder of chickens, strawberries, and hybrid corn
    and Iowa's only U.S. Vice President was born,
    on a nine-acre tract of virgin Iowa prairie
    in West of Orient I saw pink and white beardtongue

I saw where Jenny Lind and Tom Thumb appeared
    in Stone City, where Cyphert Talley, a Baptist preacher,
    was killed in the Talley or Skunk River War
    in Sigourney, where the Sac-Fox council
    started the Black Hawk War in Toolesboro,
    where Chief Wapello and his friend General Street
    are buried in the same plot along the C.B.&Q.
    right-of-way in Agency

I saw the trails worn in the sod by trekking Mormons,
    the Corning farm of Howard Townsend, historic
        communist,
    blue-eyed grass and Jerusalem artichoke,
    war clubs, knives, scrapers, grinders, and threshers,
    hickory, basswood, hackberry, wahoo, and burr,
    a Victorian parlor, a low-growing yew,
    a rare folding bathtub, a belfry stocked with birds

ALBERT GOLDBARTH *was born in Chicago, Illinois, in 1948, and has spent most of his life in that city. He received an M.F.A. from the University of Iowa in 1971, and is currently teaching creative writing at Cornell University. Poems of his have appeared in many of the country's better-known journals, and among his published books are* Coprolites *(New Rivers Press),* Opticks *(Seven Woods Press), and* Jan. 31 *(Doubleday).*

LETTER BACK TO OREGON

1

"Hello! Good luck: the trip out west blew our hair free of the city knots, and we arrived in Eugene on a sunny day. Now we are bouncing along route 5 south from Eugene to Wheatfield, California. We have 20 isosceles triangles in the bus, components of a sundome to be put up over a swimming pool. This is a new direction for us."

With nothing but such a sky to reflect
no wonder the human brain is gray.
As birds migrate far to the south
of our dreams, other thoughts
pass through our heads like bullets.
Birds here are doorstops, or stuffed in the cracks.
Ira, Chicago prepares for winter.
The Midwest hugs September and November
on either side, armed guards.

The garotte may differ
but not the cold. In some suburbs
mink collars tighten
surreptitiously against the wind.
In my neighborhood, a man could die
for want of hugging; a woman's arm
is all there ever is between my neck
and weather. It's worst at night.

Ira, Chicago prepares for winter.
We slide for love on the icy line
that separates scarves from strangulation.

We look to sparrows for how to survive.
What could I say that a sparrow hasn't
told the world with a single shrill crack
in the language of milkbottles
left on the stoop? My breath
is already white with that word.
It clatters in the pan.
We look to sparrows, to the alley-dogs.
We bury the best bones
deep in our flesh. How huge must we be
for the lake to freeze,
but the heart in the fish-ribs
keep warm at bottom? Where
to cache that one wet drop?
Ira, we walked on the lakeshore last night
and though she held my hand, the thighbones
chattered in our thighs.
It is Chicago winter; and, too cold
to swallow or even part the lips, our teeth
turn against us,
still needing meat.

The time of my life reflects the times:
the arms of women accept me
permanently no more
than turnstyles; I tell time
by departures. The time of the land
is on our wrists, is pressing
the pulse, is a watch
making circles: assassination
hasn't changed much,
some loving man crucified
on the cross-hairs. The time of the land
is divided by mountains,

is three hours long from coast to coast,
is grotesque. One midnight, clock
hand pointing up like an arrow
too late to stop the birds' migration, Ira,
we'll be in different years.

The Midwest exists under too much pressure.
Tremors, by the time they rattle
households here, exaggerate
the trembling crib, the huddling bed,
the sharp and shivering kitchen-knives.
All year, the coasts press
Lake Michigan in; and in winter,
ice even under our nails,
the lake closes in upon itself.
We look to sparrows for how to survive.
If soot is their blanket, we look to soot.
Theirs is the stationary virtue.
But tropic birds, the flamboyant, the leaders
of flocks, tell time
in their hollow bones: what enables flight,
what tells them when the time is up.
And the clock hands open
to let them rise, Ira

how are things
at the edge of the nation?
Give my regards.
Wish you were here.

2

"We are looking soon to buy land. I remembered the Indians
and eastern concept of cycles. To push our belief in sym-
bolism through—to live roundly. So we sought out dome
builders. Domes are strong, inexpensive and spiritual dwell-
ings; we're working on the sun dome now."

| The concept "bond" encompasses | *Driving from* |
| the fact of separation. What | *Mt. Rushmore,* |

is a link, if not a distance
leading from one person to another?
Even on the wedding night,
the ring keeps one band of his flesh
from hers. Even after the suicide,
the hanged man is a communication.
This is only to speak of hope,
to say that there is never loss
between Eugene and Illinois
that isn't balanced at both ends
when you exhale
and Chicago breathes in.
Where else do we find the tie that binds
if not at the end of our rope?

Where I work now, a one-armed man
serves as office receptionist,
the switchboard headphones tapping
each coast into one of his ears,
New York or Frisco, his one hand
flying among the lights and wires
so fast it's a blur, the other
flown so fast, no one can see it.
He is the man who connects us
with each other. Any day of the week
you can walk into Central Y and find him
with one arm connecting our chorus,
and one arm rummaging the hole
in the air where nothing seems to matter.
There is a progression implied by lack.
There is something symbolic in his loss
that we talk through him
faster than by letter.

a white mt. goat
ran in front
of us. We stopped,
just looked
at each other
a while.
Strange
creatures
we were
to each other.
Spent 3
nights
with Ann
and Bob
Nett: friends
of Mary-Alice's;
they've
a shack,
patchwork
barn, and 5
acres. Bob
showed me
Domebook II.
Ann collects
eggs on a
chicken ranch
for 4 hours
a day, 6 days
a week.
During those
4 hours
she picks
about
14,500

hammer, wheel, cheek, seed, typewriter keys, book, eggs
words still warm
with the touch of your palms.
By the object we know the ownership.

By the fingerprint we know the finger.
Ira, by your written words I could read
your pressing on the page, I could roll
those unravelled lines back up
and lead myself to Eugene; and find you
cuddling Mary-Alice.
Alone, in the terrible Midwest dark, hands
like mine have been known to quiver.
Each of my knuckles have battered like dice
in a tin cup. I have dipped them in that cup.
I have dropped in the cup of a handicapped man.
I have given to him, and in my fingers
weakened, as if their joints were wounds
broken into the bone. Maybe
yours too? Ira, when two friends are that scared
together, the fooled world calls it
shaking hands, a mutual quaking,
a sign of love,
a strength to channel up to the shoulders.

There is a progression implied by lack.
What any receiving end of a headset hears
as the word "newcomer,"
the point of origin, the giving end, recognizes
clearly as "ambassador" or "pioneer." Thus I look to you,
your winter still three hours away,
to tell me something incomprehensible,
some translation, what gulls recite.
I look to the coast for its view
past all boundary:
the sound
the dog hears;
the touch
at the villi;
the blue waves
washing against the visible spectrum;
the feeling of ocean
for beach;

something
of what the amputee knows,
his left arm
already in heaven.

3

"Yeah! We did it. It's 30' in diameter and 18' high covered
with 9 gauge vinyl. We didn't have a scaffold, only a 12'
ladder so the roof components were raised on long pipe
lengths and Mike stood on the ladder to bolt them, looking
like an acrobat. Eugene is a good location for optimists."

We begin losing brain cells
at age eighteen. Each day a word
sloughs off, I can feel it
by the chill thread of wind in my head.
I can feel the brain
stitched like an amnesiac's.
What weight I carry,
what small vocabulary I know best,
I say for you
with the mouth of a smokestack
where sparrows have nested
and sparrows have hatched. They're words
I stammer on your behalf.
Sometimes they fly into women's mouths
for warmth; but mostly
they shrug against frost; mostly
they hoard their Chicago themesong.
Ira, the weight you carry for me
between pines to the Pacific:
are you truly my representative?
Do you still remember the one word for blood-
binds-us-as-brothers-the-way-ocean-
nourished-bathed-and linked-
our-primal ancestors? A word
like *air* or *pain*, something shared.
That burden we sometimes feel, I think

we are all the legs of the same huge animal.
Everybody, branded alike.
Neither the fakir,
the junkie, nor the drunken sailor
feels the needle.
I think we are all one animal.
The fakir sleeps on his bed of nails,
the junkie dreams,
and the sailor wakes: with butterflies,
battleships, vipers, and showgirls
tattooed on his back.
And somewhere, what
I dreamt, what shapes the painful stabs
in my back were transformed into,
appear in the rashes and hickeys
this animal bears
on its skin,
on its transcontinental flexing.
We carry nothing so heavy as flesh.
The tightest yoke
is a neck;
the world's most foolproof shackles
are wrists.
Now the fakir without a license,
the junkie trapped in his tunneled arm,
and the sailor breaching some debutante's peace
are less closely bondaged
to their captors than to that one beast
for which they sleep, and dream, and wake;
for which their wrists are a secret chain gang.
Such handcuffs bind us
inevitably to whatever
pulse is synchronous with our own.
Whose kiss,
what fangs, which pummeling
wings whistle
one night between your shoulder blades?

Look, I think
how we each cut the x there.

The ancient Sumerians ate onions
as we eat apples; lovers breathed sweet
onionscent on lovers. Because we weren't there,
never in its entire history
did Sumerian breath stink. Ira,
the word is: *air*. Despite what you think
or write to me of the foetid skyline
entering through Chicago doors like mustard-gas
into the nostrils of doughboys, despite that
mouth in my city hall
defending an unjust war with the oxygen
your plants, green spider-plant and avocado,
leave in Chicago as a sign of your stay:
breathe deep with me. Lay down the apples
and kneel before the small green flags
on their stems; and think, when you pant
hardhard above Mary-Alice, close upon her like topsoil
spreading down roots, that love,
it is but one of may ways
two hearts can be congruent.

Everybody remembers a summer
spent leaping over creeks,
almost a flying, our bodies the constellations
fish imagined, our shadows
the fish's night. But this is winter
in the Midwest. The creek is the silver
glut of ice naked hands could freeze to.
Ira, although I must return to them,
I remove the woman's hands from mine.
My gloves go off. My blue veins glisten.
Ira and Mary-Alice Brown,
I open the pores on the palms of my hands
and breathe with my hands into Illinois;
and exhale these words with the cells of my brain:

air is what there is between us.
By distance you could not deny it.
By factories you could not pollute it.
By calling it fart you could not degrade it.
By apples and onions we keep it alive.
And now we know how fruits are sundomes,
and vegetables sundomes,
and animals sundomes
admitting light through their clearest parts.
And now the effects of sun on ice,
how I'm coming to you, through this hemisphere, already,
alright, how my hands are dissolving.

KEITH GUNDERSON, *born in* 1935, grew up in Min-
neapolis, Minnesota, while living at 3142 *Lyndale Ave. So., Apt.*
24, *an address that is the title of a prose-poem sequence published by*
the Minnesota Writers' Publishing House. His *other volume of*
poetry is A Continual Interest in the Sun and Sea *(Abelard-*
Schuman, 1971*); he has also published* Mentality and Machines
(Doubleday, 1971*). He has taught philosophy at Princeton and the*
University of California at Los Angeles, and is currently a professor
of philosophy and research associate for the Minnesota Center for
Philosophy of Science at the University of Minnesota.

NAMING THE STATE BIRD

And because we lived in a democracy all the school kids get
to vote for some bird to be The State Bird and in fact any kid
in any class in any grade except kindergarten could
nominate a candidate for The State Bird and after the voting
the results would be sent to the guys who had been elected
to run The State of Minnesota and they would figure out
democratically which bird was the lucky winner and I guess
the wood duck was or the loon but no one who was in our
class which was 8th Grade Room 205 at Jefferson Junior
High had ever even heard or thought about those birds so
they didn't get considered and there were six or seven of us
who were boys who played a lot of ball together and got in
trouble for fun so the bird we nominated our class to
nominate was THE CHICKEN and anyone in favor of a
particular class nomination could give a speech on behalf of
that bird so we all gave speeches on behalf of THE
CHICKEN and talked about eggs and eating chicken on
Sunday and what other bird did so much for everyone and
one of us questioned a guy who'd come out for THE
CARDINAL about what a cardinal could be used for and all
he could think to say was that they were red and pretty and
a baseball team was named after them so we booed and
hissed at the cardinal until the teacher said no booing or

hissing allowed and then the teacher remembered that
although she wasn't permitted to vote THE ORIOLE was
her favorite bird and probably quite a few people like THE
ORIOLE and they build such interesting nests so about two
seconds later at least five kids really liked THE ORIOLE and
nominated it even though one of them thought it was green
but we kept talking up the usefulness of THE CHICKEN
and when the votes were counted THE CHICKEN squeaked
in the winner with THE ORIOLE second as we laughed and
clapped until the teacher reminded us that laughers and
clappers could stay after school and that democracy was a
serious business and there'd be no more nonsense about
messy chickens and since THE ORIOLE came in second and
was the only SERIOUS candidate of the two it would be the
nomination of Room 205 and one that we could all be proud
of.

THE GYPSY MOTORCYCLE CLUB OF SOUTH MINNEAPOLIS

                                    gathers
                              and gathers
                            by Lake Calhoun
                          where they rev and
                          rev where they rev
                          their cycles and
                        stare at people who
                      don't have them women
                    standing tough in a sort
                  of slant semi-gorgeous with
                big tits the men out of matinee
              movies part handsome good at scorn-
            ing and loud laughing they meet to
          discuss dues or the next long trip
        but mostly just in order to be the
      club with each other the cycles the
    night and the cycles and often decide
  on a short run just for the evening
      to Hastings or Hudson or to Red Wing
        and back the men switch serious and
          adjust things their goggles and belts
            and women and straddle the cycles which
              are lavished with lights like pinballs
                a power moves into the cycles in
                  jerks like an orgasm in jerks
                    and then they gun off in
                      ones in twos in ones
                        and threes and twos
                          a black leather night
                            waits for them starry
                              with studs and a
                                wind moves by the
                                  gypsies in the
                                    shape of their
                                    scarves

JIM HARRISON, *born in 1937, lives with his wife and two daughters on a farm near Lake Leelanau in northern Michigan. He has no occupation, but has published six books, the most recent being* Letters to Yesenin *(Sumac Press) and a novel,* A Good Day to Die *(Simon & Shuster).* ["After Reading Takahashi" is dedicated to Lucien and Peter.]

I WAS PROUD . . .

I was proud at four that my father called me Little Turd of Misery.
A special name somehow connected to all the cows and horses in
the perpetual mire of the barnyard. It has a resonance to it un-
known to president senator poet septic tank cleaner critic butcher
hack or baker liberal or snot, rightist and faker and faggot and
cunt hound. A child was brought forth and he was named Little Turd
of Misery and like you was thrown into the lake to learn how to
swim, owned dogs that died stupidly but without grief. Why does
the dog chase his broken legs in a circle. He almost catches them
like we almost catch our unruly poems. And our fathers and uncles
had ordinary pursuits, hunted and fished, smelled of tobacco and
liquor, grew crops, made sauerkraut and wine, wept in the dark,
chased stray cows, mended fences, were hounded as they say by
creditors. Barns burned. Cabbages rotted. Corn died of drought
before its holy ears were formed, wheat flattened by hail and wind and
the soup grew only one potato and a piece of salt pork from its
center. Generations of slavery. All so we could fuck neurotically
and begin the day rather than end it drinking and dreaming of dead
dogs, swollen creeks with small bridges, ponds where cows are caught
and drown sucked in by the muck. But the wary boy catches fish
there, steals a chicken for his dog's monthly birthday, learns
to smoke, sees his first dirty picture and sings his first dirty
song, goes away, becomes deaf with song, becomes blinded by love,
gets letters from home but never returns. And his nights become less black
and holy, less moon blown and sweet. His brain burns away like
gray parafin. He's tired. His parents are dead or he is dead
to his parents. He smells the smell of a horse. The room is
cold. He dims the lights and builds a noose. It works too well.

TODAY WE'VE MOVED . . .

Today we've moved back to the granary again and I've annointed
the room with Petrouchka. Your story, I think. And music. That
ends with you floating far above in St. Petersburg's blue winter
air, shaking your fist among the fish and green horses, the dim-
inutive yellow sun and a chicken playing the bass drum. Your
sawdust is spilled and you are forever borne by air. A simple story.
Another madman, Nijinsky, danced your part and you danced his.
None of us apparently is unique. Think of dying waving a fist full
of ballpoint pens that change into small snakes and that your
skull will be transposed into the cymbal it was always meant to be.
But shall we come down to earth? For years I have been too ready
to come down to earth. A good poet is only a sorcerer bored with
magic who has turned his attention elsewhere. O let us see wonders
that psilocybin never conceived of in her powdery head. Just now
I stepped on a leaf that blew in the door. There was a buzzing
and I thought it concealed a wasp, but the dead wasp turned out to be
a tiny bird, smaller than a hummingbird or june bug. Probably one
of a kind and I can tell no one because it would anger the swarm
of naturalists so vocal these days. I'll tuck the body in my hair
where it will remain forever a secret or tape it to the back of
your picture to give you more depth than any mirror on earth.
And another oddity: the record needle stuck just at the point
the trumpet blast announced the appearance of your ghost in the
form of Petrouchka. I will let it repeat itself a thousand times
through the afternoon until you stand beside the desk in your
costume. But I've no right to bring you back to life. We must
respect your affection for the rope. You knew the exact juncture
in your life that the act of dangling could be made a dance.

AFTER READING TAKAHASHI

Nothing is the same to anyone.
Moscow is east of Nairobi
but thinks of herself as perpetually west.
The bird sees the top of my head,
an even trade for her feathered belly.
Our eyes staring through the nose bridge
never to see each other.
She is not I, I not her.
So what, you think, having little
notion of my concerns. O that dank
basement of "so what" known by all
though never quite in the same way.
All of us drinking through a cold afternoon,
our eyes are on the mirror behind
the bottles, on the snow out the window
which the wind chases fruitlessly,
each in his separateness drinking,
talk noises coming out of our mouths.
In the corner a pretty girl plays pinball.
I have no language to talk to her.
I have come to the point in life when
I could be her father. This was never true before.
The bear hunter talked about the mountains.
We looked at them together out of the
tavern window in Emigrant, Montana.
He spent fifty years in the Absaroka Mountains
hunting grizzly bears and at one time, wolves.
We will never see the same mountains.
He knows them like his hands, his wife's
breasts and legs, his old dog sitting outside
in the pickup. I only see beautiful mountains
and say "beautiful mountains" to which he nods
graciously but they are a photo of China to me.

And all lessons are fatal: the great snowy owl
that flew in front of me so that
I ducked in the car; it will never happen again.
I've been warned by a snowy night, an owl,
the infinite black above and below me to look
at all creatures and things with a billion eyes,
not struggling with the single heartbeat
that is my life.

WILLIAM HARROLD, *born in 1936, lives in Milwaukee, Wisconsin, and teaches English and creative writing at the University of Wisconsin–Milwaukee. He received the 1973 North Carolina Poetry Council Award for* Beyond the Dream, *and his critical work* The Variance and the Unity: A Study of the Complementary Poems of Robert Browning *was published in 1973 by Ohio University Press.*

A SMALL TRIBUTE

An arsonist of flesh,
I set your heart on fire.
That was twenty years ago.

And the tongue that dissolved your face
Still pants among the briars.

I have seen children with no mouths
Sledding your breasts
Into the nameless flowers
And have come with all the singers
To pay tribute in silence.

Now I leave you in your chair
Fumbling at something near your hairline.
You feel once more, currying back
Through the days with your shell comb.

It is not the hearing aid that troubles you,
Dangling like a pearl along your shoulder.
It is only my ruffled feathers frozen in your ear.
I know it's useless now to tell you.
I was coming inside with my song.

ANOTHER LOAD

They haul away our nights in manure trucks.
Here in this house we sit finishing the season,
you rocking your six cheap diamonds,
me watering blue ideas on the child's grave.
The mirror in the hallway reflects the record,
two lovers pressed like puritans on an ironing board.
only one black prayer wing still flapping.
You stir your finger in my blood
looking for lost leeches and come
again to the place where you cracked me,
pain running out on spider's feet
walls closing up like poisonous flowers.

FLOWERS FOR THE GRANGERFORD GIRL

Emmiline, you were there even before they were cold,
your ears always listening for the final breath.
The neighbors, sometimes years short of forty,
must have felt rushed by the ram of your sharp pen.
Where are you now when death sweats
like a rainy day on the lazy Mississippi?
You were last seen bending above some
flowers as the sun fell into Kansas.
I'd guess you've seen Miss Watson's Lord
and often write your finest Sheaffer
odes on paper thin as blackbird's breath.

MICHAEL HEFFERNAN *was born in Detroit, Michigan, in* 1942. *He received his B.A. in English from the University of Detroit, and, as a Woodrow Wilson Fellow, studied at the University of Massachusetts, where he earned a doctorate in* 1970 *with his work on William Carlos Williams's* Paterson. *He has published poems in leading periodicals, and a short collection of his work,* Booking Passage, *appeared in* 1973. *He lives in Pittsburg, Kansas, where he teaches at Kansas State College and serves as poetry editor of* Midwest Quarterly.

IN BLESSED WEATHER

The light comes into the house and a few flies
stumble from light to shadow and again to light
where chairs and a table sit and the Armstrong floor

is clusters of squares among rectangles
lifting up bits of light, and the pair of chairs
that were my uncle's that died of a wintry life

edge up to my grandmother's table
that no longer looks like the table where I sat
in front of her Sunday suppers because my wife

decided to strip it down to the bare wood
one Saturday in the fall. One of the chairs
is altogether in shadow and the other

has one of its back rungs brightened by sunshine
while nothing more than a narrow lance of light
aims under it over the darkling squares

and a cat whose hair is black and white
treads into the place I'm in
oblivious of this light, not even knowing the sun

has been drawn down into its deeps
behind our air and circumstance and weather
or that I am sitting here being the bard

reminding this place and every one of you
that I know where I am and that I do
precisely what I do because I do it
because I am the poet

that saw the dog that fled through my neighbor's yard
an instant ago so fast I would have had to
disrupt my train of thought to have said so
exactly when he did so

and because the flies still tumble into the light from some-
   where
and the table and chairs are still and the cat reclines
with both paws extended over an arm of a chair made of
   wicker

opening his face to yawn
onto the light that comes all the way from the sun
to his twenty-one whiskers and all his hairs and claws

on a sunporch seven miles inside Kansas
at the end of October
in blessed weather.

A FIGURE OF PLAIN FORCE

You let the door sway open on its hinges
Into a cleansing quiet where the sunlight
Moves in the air like seawash among cool windows
And beyond them a stretch of open country
That strives into the sea. You have begun
Nothing of consequence yet, though you may begin

By desperate measures something you left undone
Or went to do and quit remembering.
In this condition you pretend to lean
Solidly into the open while you gather
The winds about you by deliberate grace,
Turning you into a figure of plain force,
Careful and candid, never in a dither,
Given to nothing noisome or unclean.

THE APPARITION

Trying to get the whiskey to do it and after that
Lumbering out in the yard for a stray dog or a spook
Shambling from nowhere: as you pause, consider the flat
Gut of Orion, taut as a boxer's, how he took
Some bobcat's hair off with his bare hands
And for a time you're happy, having read that in no book.
Then you stroll back in like a man who demands
Intensity, haul down the liquor for a last try
And the kitchen's surly again like a crowd of urchins,
So you swagger to bed then, leave them alone
To dwindle behind you in the dry dark while
Whatever it was that whitened inside you — bone
Or guardian angel — gathers up stair by stair
Into the grisliest of apparitions,
Staying your passage further into no more air.

TOM HENNEN *was born in Morris, Minnesota, in* 1942, *and grew up on farms in the surrounding area. He lives now in Stevens County, Minnesota, with his wife and two children. Hennen has had poems in* New Letters, The Seventies, *and* Straight Creek Journal. *His first volume of poetry,* The Heron with No Business Sense, *was recently published by the Minnesota Writers' Publishing House.*

MINNEAPOLIS

Blackened trees
Limbless from industrial accidents
Huddle on the outskirts of the city.

The swamp has become a supermarket overnight.
A heron with no business sense
Vanishes.

The hungry man from the woods
Feeds on loose change
Like a parking meter.

At night
The smokestacks sink into the prairie.
Underground the soot changes hands.
The night shift moves slowly
Emitting a dim light from their mole eyes.

An odor of small lakes
Survives in the clothing of insects.

SMELLING A STONE IN THE MIDDLE OF WINTER

I can't remember
What gravel and weeds look like.
This little stone becomes important
And starts to act big.
I expect it to orbit the kitchen stove
Any minute now.
Near my nose
It gets
Bigger and bigger
Until it's a mountain
I'm lost on.

This stone is different
Than the stone that grinds me down
All day
At work.

This stone
Smells like the inside of your dress
On a spring afternoon.
It's the hard feeling in my stomach
When I'm talking nonsense to you.

This stone is so inviting
Everyone wants to walk right into it
And become a fossil.

DIRT ROAD

A feather plucked out and tossed away
By an old bird.
Shells of bugs
Whose names I don't know

Crunch
No matter where I put my feet.

After walking hard all summer
A goose voice
Tells me
I've caught up with autumn.

JOB HUNTING

I want a job as a low cloud
Heavy as my wet wool cap
So if I'm hit
By lightning on the hill
I won't have to explain being out so late
Or how my socks got damp.

In the early morning I'll hang
Over evergreen branches
My ear lappers down
As lights go on
In the bedrooms
Alarm clocks ringing like words
Of the first awake.

Almost frozen
I drift sideways
Across the sky
Rain turning to snow.

THE NEW ARM

We all have
A new arm
Growing outward
From the shoulder
Filled with bullets.
It is leading us
Into continents
Where the people
Are disguised as colored maps.

We will sink
Arm first
To the bottom of liquid countries.

Many years from now
Some of us
Will surface in Asia
As white roots
Between cows' teeth,
And some of us
Will appear near our homes
With heavy arms we can't lift,
Making noises
On the wooden siding.

GOING INTO THE WOODS

I see your breath
In mid-air
Like a cloud
Hiding mosquitoes
Still lakes
Hot nights
You and me

Without clothes.
Wife, when you breathe the world fills up.

Let's go into the woods.
I'll listen
To your lungs take in red leaves
Snow
Goose bumps
And the call of the freight train
Migrating south.

Let's lay here for awhile
So still
That everyone will take us for rocks.

OLD FOLKS HOME

On shadowy back porches
Rocking chairs
Are still
As fallen trees.

The old
Are
Imprisoned
In those bomb shelters
I see on the edge
Of prairie towns.

Strapped down
For a long voyage
They can't tell us anything
But only orbit
Far out in the gloom
Forever.

THOMAS JAMES, *to whose memory this volume is in part dedicated, was born in Illinois in 1946, and died in 1974. He studied at Northern Illinois University, then taught for some time in Joliet, Illinois. He also wrote fiction, and he was a good actor.* James won the Theodore Roethke Prize, *from* Poetry Northwest, *in 1969, and he published in a number of magazines, including* Poetry, Epoch, *and* North American Review. *His volume of poetry* Letters to a Stranger *was published by Houghton Mifflin in 1973.*

TIMOTHY

You loved me because I brought you sugar cubes
Stolen at breakfast, dropped into my trousers
Furtively, under the flowered oilcloth.
Your nose a prickle at my knucklebones,
I watched leafshadows skittering like mice
Over your body's warm, incredible silk.

I brought you a bouquet of mustard flowers
Drenched in the morning dew, its bone-white lights,
And you ate it. I stood for hours, lonely,
Knee-deep in your bruised blue shadow,
The wire between us charged with tiny currents
That kept you hostage in your sunny meadow.

My grandmother told me death begins like this:
Stalled in the shadow of a horse, with morning
Breaking its lights around you. Before the summer vanished
The crickets stood up in their polished armor,
The milkweed stirred inside its knobby wardrobe.
My bones began to push against my skin.

In your kind eyes the summer broke itself:
Armloads of daisies, spikes of chicory,
The far-off chiming of the field frogs,
A ditch of Queen Anne's lace turned ragged

Flickered and burned away into each eye hole,
The displaced landscape anchored in your skull.

Inside your eyes I am a child, Timothy!
A small, inert reflection blooms and fades
Against those lilac-shaded surfaces —
A child smaller than a melting snowflake
Stretches his arms to you, one full of sweetness,
The other fountaining with yellow flowers.

SPIDER IN THE GRAPES

I crouch among the arbor's swollen tongues:
They are the size of someone's thumb,
Blunt, oval shapes the color of carbon paper,
Casketed in shawls of smooth white dust.
Numb and forgetful, I observe the grape leaves.
They are brown as rust, in need of some mending —

I fashion tight cocoons to patch their raggedness,
And they endure. I squat among them,
Leveling my gaze on the horizons.
They seem to fray themselves night after night
As if they were not sure of their importance.
By dawn they will be wan as tarnished pewter.

Holding a small, precarious light,
By noon the sky will knit its minor fractures.
Another season is hammering it into mica.
Is this light the sum of what I know?
Even the flies have broken me —
Their little wings dangle like washed-out leaves.

In the torn cradles of my ruptured village.
The gnats steer off, busy with their offspring,
Fragile, elusive. The stars do not console me.

I long for a light impermanent as sunrise,
The shimmer of dragonflies after rain,
Clear drops of water silvering the grapeskins.

Tongues fit to burst, the grapes are harboring messages,
Their lusters peeling off. Do they contain the dark?
Frost has begun to lap the arbor's slats.
Tonight I'll wind myself in spools of silk,
Guarding the egg sac, all my frail belongings,
And shut my eyes before the sky grows faceless.

TOM O' BEDLAM AMONG THE SUNFLOWERS

To have gold in your back yard and not know it . . .
I woke this morning before your dreams had shredded
And found a curious thing: flowers made of gold,

Six-sided — more than that — broken on the flagstones,
Petals the color of a wedding band.
You are sleeping. The morning comes up gold.

Perhaps I made those flowers in my head,
For I have counted snowflakes in July
Blowing across my eyes like bits of calcium,

And I have stepped into your dreams at night,
A stranger there, my body steeped in moonlight.
I watched you tremble, washed in all that silver.

Love, the stars have fallen into the garden
And turned to frost. They have opened like a hand.
It is the color that breaks out of the bedsheets.

This morning the garden is littered with dry petals
As yellow as the page of an old book.
I step among them. They are brittle as bone china.

I enter your dreams this way. I am your burglar.
I hoard the things I take out of your sleep,
I walk your dreams till I become those dreams —

The last sunflowers turn to the sun and brighten.
You are sleeping. Now the window drains its indigos.
Your dreams unravel in the chilly room.

I reach for one last bloom. A palmful of gold.
The morning star is eaten by the distance.
I stand in the spikes of frost, a lunatic.

LOUIS JENKINS *was born in Oklahoma City, Oklahoma, in* 1942. *He lives now in Duluth, Minnesota, where he teaches a poetry class at a local high school and edits* Steelhead, *a magazine of poetry. He has published poems in* Crazy Horse, Dacotah Territory, Hawaii Review, Lamp in the Spine, The Seventies, *and other magazines. He is the author of* The Well Digger's Wife, *a chapbook of twenty poems published by the Minnesota Writers' Publishing House.*

PORTAGE POEM

First the canoe,
400 rods over a hilly trail,
then back for the packs
and the fishing poles
and one last look at the lake.

I wish it would always be like this.
Move up, go back,
pick everything up,
leave nothing
but the pines,
the lake,
the fall afternoon.

LIBRARY

I sit down at a table and open a book of poems and move slowly into the shadows of tall trees. They are white pines I think. The ground is covered with soft brown needles and there are signs that animals have come here silently and vanished before I could catch sight of them. But here the trail edges into a cedar swamp; wet ground, deadfall and rotting leaves. I move carefully but rapidly, pleased with myself.

Someone else comes and sits down at the table, a serious looking young man with a large stack of books. He takes a book from the top of the stack and opens it. The book is called *How to Get a High Paying Job*. He flips through it and lays it down and picks up another and pages through it quickly. It is titled *Moving Ahead*.

We are moving ahead very rapidly now, through a second growth of popple and birch, our faces scratched and our clothes torn by the underbrush. We are moving even faster now, marking the trail, followed closely by bulldozers and crews with chain saws and representatives of the paper company.

MEDICINE

He sits in the chair and does not move for a long time. He thinks he should do something, take some action, but he doesn't know what. Nothing seems worth the effort. He leans his head back to rest against the wall, stretches out his legs and is still again, not quite asleep. The way he sits he seems a part of something else. One side of a mountain perhaps, the way it slopes down to flat land. This year the crops burned up, livestock died. The land is cracked and dry. The little girl is sick. The wife no longer speaks and lies down each night beside the child. The farmer walks out to look at the sky, his hands limp at his sides, followed by a skinny dog. It grows dark. The moon rises making a shadowy light on the trail. A thin man dressed in black sits easily in the saddle. He is the man from the medicine show, bringing his bottles down from the mountains. Bottles of pure water. With each careful step of the pony the bottles in the saddle bags clink together. The man is singing quietly to himself.

A QUIET PLACE

I have come to understand my love for you. I came to you like a man, world weary, looking for a quiet place. The gas station and grocery store, the church, the abandoned school, a few old houses, the river with its cool shady spots, good fishing. How I've longed for a place like this! I've searched the country for months, years looking for just the right place. As soon as I got here I knew I'd found it. Tomorrow the set production crew and the film crew arrive. We can begin filming on Friday: the story of a man looking for a quiet place.

JOHN JUDSON, *born in 1930, currently teaches English at the University of Wisconsin–La Crosse, where he also edits* Voyages to the Inland Sea, *a series of books devoted to the work of midwestern poets. His most recent book is* Finding Words in Winter *(Elizabeth Press), and poems of his have appeared in over 200 literary magazines. He lives in La Crosse, between Hedgehog Bluff and the Mississippi River, with his wife and three children.*

24 *DECEMBER*

from "Diary of a Lone Cold"
For those with empirical
    experience of altitude, twice
        the distance between

the bottom and the middle
    is up. It is
        the morning before

Christmas. Tonight we
    will work late,
        singing softly to

ourselves, having a drink
    or two, thinking back
        to the thirties and

before, to virgin birth,
    while outside the window,
        snow and the landscape's

clarity will keep us
    this American distance
        from each other, as

alien as the Burlington's
    1:15 freight, me-
        andering down the valley

of the Father of the Waters,
   hauling our northern
      currents south,

so that in imagination,
   at least, we can
      meet the sea,

dropping our mortgages, our
   time, our flesh
      to face its blue

mystery, as hungry fishermen
   would unfold their nets,
      hoping to gather

in one bright and tightened
   string, a standard
      measure of ourselves.

FINDING WORDS IN WINTER

I *thursday:* 4:30 *p.m.*

a)
Soft light, low
   light, the
      barns extinguish

themselves, their
   red goes home,
      absorbs into crows'

blood, lurches where
   the late horizon
      leans against the

River. Now they take
   flight, move, bark; their
      wings black within me.

b)

I will feed on the speech of animals,
on fur that colors me winter,
my eyes gray,
numb as the soft edge of words
that drift the roads
prowling Nebraska's wind.

II *friday:* 8:30 *a.m.*

Smoke drifts south
   along the roofs
      of Main Street's large

white houses, their
   sunporches and eaves
      heavy-lipped, iced

with last week's snow.
   I hear no birds
      but the sound of

a typewriter clicking
   like gravel
      against the pane

of my window: my
   keys at their usual
      winter hunt and

peck, dribbling
   a clear line of
      seed or sorrow.

This portable black
   machine that leads me by
      a ribbon that is

creased and pounded
   beyond all symmetry,
      bent to experience

by the weight
   of my quiet tongue,
      by black crevices

between my teeth,
   the odor of morning
      breath, the lines and

plots in the aerial
   photographs of my
      dreams; why it

is not music,
   only my soul
      can know; it

keeps me
   in its dark: here
      there are no birds,

only flat morning
   moving in these lines
      and snow.

III *franciscan ode for small birds*

Little children, suffer
   to know poems,
      for they are like

the fisherman
   who lost his oldest
      daughter in a car

wreck, whose mind is
   crying behind a
      quiet face and

tired eyes, but
   who can talk to you,
      occasionally, with

great joy,
   telling of sunsets
      when the trout are rising.

They feed time
   and small birds;
      they are free

supplies of cracked seed
   on plain boards
      in sun behind houses,

and in this land,
   suet for
      our winter's singing.

IV *over the viaduct:* 8:08 *a.m.*

Be-
   hind every word,
      a train,

pushing,
   clearing the weight
      of new snow,

huffing the down
  out and away,
    checking in on

time, exact as
  a librarian,
    or this morning

flat on the sky,
  the dime of
    sun

blurred: an
  artist's judgement,
    paint smeared by

the speed of
  his thumb,
    by the speed

thought makes
  as it lights
    part of him.

V *hike on the bluffs*

Nine o'clock is many metaphors;
it is also morning,
the quality of light
I live with:
boots through crusted snow to rock,
to where the last pine leans,
out of breath at the ridge top,
at the wind's end.

Morning is here,
there is no qualifying;
it qualifies me,

the melt of snow,
the girdle of rain
or the autumn fogs I've been clouded in,
swept like dust out
from under her skirt.

VI

*Primarily the house consists of two suits of fur, worn one
over the other, and each carefully tailored to the wearer's di-
mensions. The inner suit works with the hair of the hides fac-
ing inward and touching the skin while the outer suit has its
hair turned out to the weather.*
FARLEY MOWAT IN *People of the Deer*

Even our best friends
are strangers who
read poems.

This constant
urban chafing in
forced hot air,

behind shrubs that
bothways
block the view,

against exhaust
from cars warming
up mornings or

Cruisers all night
crunching
the snow;

all these
make the heart
callous, the

poem thick-
skinned. It
must turn

again,
keep its fur
inward.

VII

Song Cousin, brother of the Caribou, Ihalmiut never met,
I write out of my winter's dark,
knowing your house of snow block sawed on a slant
is my best metaphor yet.

Cousin, take this, my brightest necktie as a gift,
put it in your amulet to keep from choking on us.
In this cold, our houses creak, our windows sweat.

VIII *the chaperone's Much Ado . . .*

Whirled, the world learns to balance itself between poles,
changing with each season,
but fall clings with the scent of blood to its bones,
like the old Bear, Cousin to the Eskimo, Wanderer,
who in all white likelihood shapes a trail direct,
keeps fur between him and any stray wind.

Instead, we wear a bus.
Whirled, our tires slip against crushed rain
turned ice before light this morning.
We, in a steel skin, with 20 people from another spring
who nod and smile, reading alien maps of themselves:
Koppit's INDIANS
FOR WHOM THE BELL TOLLS
THE KENNEDY YEARS.

I squeeze your hand and counter them,
look into the only galaxy of gray
hair for a stretch of 16 seats,
thinking ahead to the Guthrie where
Shakespeare's frenzied eye rolls nightly off the stage,
gathering the audience up as one
before it breaks itself with a laugh.

Outside the Mississippi bluffs slip by,
their high springs frozen huge and round,
tinted a Mediterranean blue
by impurities in Minnesota limestone.
Their ice stands like ancient shields
parrying shafts of the sun,
scattering them beneath our wheels.

Whirled, the poem in me learns.

IX *spring comes to hedgehog bluff*

Eye moves up the incline,
traces the slow melt of spring,
crosses the road behind
grapevine, burning bush, red dogwood,
zigzagging on the steep bluff-side,
following a trail of least resistance
around elm, birch, juniper shrub,
making its way to the top
above low birds and suburbs.

The thin black shattered road
that holds us all together.
Nothing redeemed.
No ancient Chinese spirit
here. Only a full
view of cities,
which all heights must
come down to.

STANLEY KIESEL, *born in Los Angeles, California, in 1925, taught kindergarten for seventeen years. He has also worked as a poet in schools in Illinois and South Dakota, and at present is poet-in-residence for the Minneapolis, Minnesota, public schools. His book of poems* The Pearl Is a Hardened Sinner *was published by Scribner's in 1968, and his work has appeared in* The Nation, Antioch Review, The New Republic, *and other periodicals.*

A FAREWELL

Partner in the corner bar is high, a grin
Scratched on her face. In effigy, her smile,
On the wet counter, guards her lost senses.
Alcohol's her diary; her factory; gallery of all
The pictures in her head; the inclined plane
Down which slide all the children of her need.

I know what makes her eyes foam up: a cruel
Sliver in her mind's finger; the Morse Code
Of her sex begging to move, to be gratified;
Italicized from the beginning, it never lied.
O how this knowledge swings back and fro!

Love-affair flies up like a football
For someone to catch; for someone to stick
Pins of sense into and compound. Not for our
Own understanding apparently, was it born.
Who can survey this ground, wrestle with this
Affinity, hold its shoulders down,
Blueprint the impression it leaves on the grass?

Sometimes I think an embrace is like a mine field
Where pleasure is torn apart; that what
We think of as love is simply a breakwater
To keep our rage intact. Gaze up at the moon
Of indiscretion . . . it pleases; and yet
How worthless it is, hardly a mat to sleep on;
A turd stuck with primroses;
And so we prink up—what?—and call it love.

From this avant-garde boulevard room a bell
Of logic tolls. And now comes the time
To take discretion's temperature, to harness tact;
To spear the little pink deceits. Sliding down
The bannisters of a joke, bestowing medals
On her own inspiration, she comes. Tonight,
In her glance's palm, I'll read of the downtrodden
Haste of her life, watch her unbox all the
Different puzzle pieces of her disposition;
Her worship of love crawls like a baby,
Is almost pitiful in its naked need, one would
Spread out for it the tablecloth of perfection.

Face, do not refuse counsel.
Listen. Who can eventually
Pickpocket the world? Neither
You nor I. These sad
Words blot with the morning.

Poor disheveled ringleader,
There is no bottle of force
Can make love last; or
Impulse that will not be
Later torn for rags;
Or statue melted down
But will do its own self harm.

POEM FOR MOTHER'S DAY

What goes on
in your gray matter

is beyond me.
It must always

be snowing
there, in your head.

Behind your eyes,
I know it is the worst

winter in years.
There, in your head,

in the drifts,
a thousand struck matches

cannot make you
warm. I

am one of those
matches,

so I know.
One day, the snow

will pile up too high.
Even the headlines

won't be able
to find you.

That day,
I shall rush out

from my books,
naked, illiterate,

tearing to pieces
my library card,

crying, Mama! Mama!
today, I will

play basketball!
Today, I will

give you my
gym shorts to wash!

Today, I will even forget
to marry my wife!

DON'T PUT ME

Don't put me
In a home
When I am old,
You said.
Don't put me
In a room
With those
Who are only
Holes.

And then,
Remembering
Your own mother,
Whom you left
Among the
Walking dead
With only
A brush and comb,
Drops of guilt
Fell down.
Drops,
Into your lap,
Which no son
For forty years
Has sat upon.

Senile, she was,
You said.
She burnt her
Pots, she couldn't
Smell gas. She
Wandered. Samaritans

Drove her home.
(Down to the rug:
Drops)
Don't put me,
You said,
With crazies.

Drops. And in
Those drops
I saw, Mother,
Your mother.
In every drop,
Felt again
That last
Grip when,
From that gross
Room, brush
And comb had
Gone.

Drops. Drops
You now cry,
Mother, for you.
Don't put me, you
Say. Do I
Hear you?
That's your torture.
Do I truly
Hear you?
That's what
Money's for,
Isn't it?
That's what one
Saves for,
Isn't it?
From being put?
From being put.

Well Mother.
I hear you.
The drops
Are shrewd.
In every
Drop, Mother,
Your mother
Says:
Don't put me;
Takes my hand, says:
Don't put me.
Bravo, Mother.
The drops
Are masterpieces.

TED KOOSER *was born in Ames, Iowa, in 1939. His first collection of poetry,* Official Entry Blank, *was published in 1969 by the University of Nebraska Press, and his poems have appeared in many literary magazines. He lives in Lincoln, Nebraska, where he is employed as an underwriter in the home office of an insurance company. Kooser is the editor of the* New Salt Creek Reader, *a literary quarterly.*

A PLACE IN KANSAS

for Jon Gierlich

Somewhere in Kansas, a friend found
an empty stone house alone in a wheatfield,
and over the door was incised a ship's anchor.
There was no one to ask
what an anchor was doing in Kansas;
not a single white sail of a meaning
broke the horizon, though he waited for hours.
It's like that in Kansas, forever.

DEEP IN WINTER

twenty new sparrows
shake out of the dustmop.

All week in the wheatfields,
the snow has been turning to bread.

I PUT MY HAND ON HIS HEAD

I put my hand on my son's head
and grow suddenly older.

His skull is heavy and sun-warmed—
a stone from a lost field,

an unopened geode,
crowded with beautiful crystals.

THE GOLDFISH FLOATS

The goldfish floats to the top of his life
and turns over, a shaving from somebody's hobby.
So it is that men die at the whims of great companies,
their neckties pulling them speechless into machines,
their wives finding them slumped in the shower
with their hearts blown open like boiler doors.
In the night, again and again these men float
to the tops of their dreams to drift back
to their desks in the morning. If you ask them,
they all would prefer to have died in their sleep.

THE BLIND ALWAYS COME AS SUCH A SURPRISE

The blind always come as such a surprise,
suddenly filling an elevator
with a great white porcupine of canes,
or coming down upon you in a noisy crowd
like the eye of a hurricane.
The dashboards of cars stopped at crosswalks
and the shoes of commuters on trains
are covered with sentences
struck down in mid-flight by the canes of the blind.
Each of them changes our lives,
tapping across the bright circles of our ambitions
like cracks traversing the favorite china.

PHONING MY SON LONG DISTANCE

Surely I know that
my voice has grown small in his house,
drawn thin by the wire,
a fly's whine in the clutter of breakfast,
a thin line of ants
winding out of a crack in the past
toward the sweet, impossible cup of his ear.

In the background, my former wife is whispering.
I clutch at the phone like a hand held down.
It grows more difficult for me
to crawl into the hot cardboard fort of his love
simply by calling on Sundays.

NORBERT KRAPF *was born in Jasper, Indiana, in 1943. He received degrees from Saint Joseph's College (Indiana) and the University of Notre Dame, and he taught in England on a Fulbright exchange. His poems have appeared in* Poetry, Kansas Quarterly, Western Humanities Review, Prism, *and* Prospice. *In England, he published a broadsheet,* Shooting a Squirrel *(Sceptre, 1973), and he has finished a volume of poems, "Back Roads." He is currently teaching at the C. W. Post Center of Long Island University.*

DARKNESS COMES TO THE WOODS

It begins to trickle
silently onto the floor
of the far side
of the woods which
the hunter cannot see.
First the creatures
dogpaddle in it, then
turn and float on their
backs as it creeps up
the bark of trees, pressing
down heavier and harder
on everything below.
Eventually the hunter
hears it lapping, then
breaking, then thundering
toward him. He turns
his back, splashes to
the field outside, looks
back on pairs of glowing
eyes gliding below
the surface of pitch—
black waters which have
swollen to the treetops.

SKINNING A RABBIT

I rip off
bobtail
pull fur
down back
peeling it
over belly
yank it
over head
across paws
drop it on
old newspaper
insert knife
where naked legs
spread apart
slash down
thru tender belly
as thin blood
drip drips
& guts bulge
stick hand
into slit
grab handfuls
of warm guts
which I tear
from back
chop head & paws
off with hatchet
plop whole wad
on top of fur
wrap corners
of newspaper
around bloody mess
compress it
into ball
to bury in garden

drop leftover flesh
in pail of water—

staring down
at a shrivelled
pink embryo
in reddening water
I blink to
the large streaking blur
my shotgun
blasted so still
& wonder why
I pulled the trigger
with such fever
the knife
with such relish
the guts
with such satisfaction.

GREG KUZMA *was born in 1944. He lives with his wife and two children in Crete, Nebraska, and teaches poetry writing workshops at the University of Nebraska. In the basement of his home he prints the poetry magazine* Pebble, *and The Best Cellar Press series of poetry pamphlets. A volume of his poetry,* Good News, *was published by Viking Press in 1973.*

GARDEN REPORT

Carrots are disappointing.
They won't take root
or hold once they do set,
and the cucumbers,
launched on little hills,
can't weather the wind
which blows them over
breaking their skin-white
stalks. Only the Indian
Corn, the only thing
we can't eat, defies
everything, even the
rabbits, grows tough and
wide as fenceposts, whips
in the wind like ropes.
The worst rain makes it
greener.

GREENS

They have stood long in the sun,
and their roots are tight screws
in the soil. They know what to
suck up, they steal all the best
from the ground. How dark their

leaves, how bitter. At dinner
we lean over them like starving men,
like men lost on a great hot ocean.
We are eating the sails of our ships,
long wasted by water.

MELONS

I have put my time into the ground.
I have stood with the hoe
and bent my back. I have dripped
in the sun like a leaf. Late nights,
with other work to do, I have
stood with the hose, a swarm of bugs
around my head. It has done me good.
An aching back, a summer gone before
my eyes like smoke, old friends
neglected, new ones in the striving
awkward plants. No writing done.
Who would have thought the growing
should take so long, that a handful
of seeds should come forth as a
full blown field, with problems
of its own. It broke my summer
into dirt and sweat, weeds and worms.
I suffered both the morning and
the evening vigils. I gave half
my crop to the birds. I worried
the drought with the peas, I
anguished in the heat that stood
above the ground and everything that
had no feet to run away knocked down.
And even in the cooled off nights
I burned.

THE WEAK

So much that is weak has survived
and lives out its long wondrous days
with only the least of annoyance.
The grim and holy, the loud and reckless,
pass them, making their great surface
disruptions. So much that is weak and
slight has bloomed beneath the dark brow
of the storm. Rage, rage, or whisper,
everything fades. The tall trees of the
yard, the small dry walnut shells.

POPPIES

Just weeks ago dead.
Just weeks ago ripped out,
the tall gangly stalks,
naked pistils, dry brown
leaves about the base,
a shambles on the hills,
and summer nearly done with here.
Already the scattered seeds
take root and rise,
have risen just this week
while we're about our
limpings and our fires,
our closings down, spectacular
new growth to shatter our
old rhythms! They are so late,
so early, breaking our sober
stride, sending us into our
things and out of ourselves
once more, so late or
early we cannot tell either—
this year the first year

that we've noticed.
How things amaze us,
how easily our orders break,
our measures shatter at the
slightest turn. How we
do not see anything, how
we do not understand, how
we are not well read in
the good book of the earth.
Oh on the hillside in the
last of August they are
coming once again.

LAURENCE LIEBERMAN *was born in* 1935. *His first volume of poems,* The Unblinding, *was published by Macmillan in* 1968, *and his second,* The Osprey Suicides, *appeared in* 1973. *His work has been widely anthologized, and his poems and critical essays have appeared in many of the country's leading magazines, including* The New Yorker, *the* Atlantic Monthly, Harper's, *and others. He is a professor of English at the University of Illinois, where he was awarded a creative writing fellowship by the Center for Advanced Study in* 1971.

A DREAM OF LAKES

Somewhere in the quiet lakes
Of Michigan fish jump every minute.
I dream of a winding shallow

Where I set up camp on the shore
And the fish jump three and four
At a time. I never catch one.

But I feel the life in that stream
Splashing about my ears,
Gill-blues and sunfish-yellows

Kicking the air like horses
Kick up dust on a track,
So many, unhungry and playful,

They bump my bait with their sides,
Their eel-slippery tails crossing
And catching my line, not to tease me,

Perhaps, but simply to let me
Know they know I am here,
Can even pretend to approve

The business of hooks and weights
In a world that lets them in on it
And makes them be cautious on purpose

With a care bred of many years slaughter,
Call it a fish-racial mourning
Of war-dead, and a birth of a fish

Sixth-sense, not to say a forgiveness
Of the enemy, me, in love
With the sound of my spinning reel

As it feeds out the end of a cast
Or hums with a slower winding
And clicks the ratchet as I reel in

A disappointing weed
Or the loose end torn from the snag
Which I mutter is fish-sabotage . . .

Often as I troll rough waters
At sea, and haul in five pounds
Every minute on my shark-tested tackle

I feel like a man in a brothel
Who gave over a delicate catch
Or the intricate mysteries of search,

Illusion, depth, expectation
Unanswered for the safe return.
I reach back for the less-assured,

The long-sought (out-of-reach, out-of-bounds),
A speckled illusion in shallows,
The splash of many tails at the surface.

R I C H A R D   L Y O N S , *born in Detroit, Michigan, in* 1920, *has taught at North Dakota State University since* 1950. *His recent poetry and fiction have appeared in* The Nation, North Country Anvil, Ann Arbor Review, South Dakota Review, Dacotah Territory, *and others magazines.* Public Journal, 1941–1971 *(Scopecraeft Press, 1972) was his fifth book.*

MEDORA, N.D.

The sleepy little village
nestled against the colored hills,
dying with its gone time,
drying away now
in a dehydrating chamber
of twentieth century speed.

Then came someone, looking,
glowing inwardly, saying,
"Let's revive the way it was,
bring back the old West,
including its muddy coffee."

So he scraped and built,
tore down and re-erected,
varnished, neoned an image,
and imported souvenirs
of cowboys, Indians, and Teddy
economically from Japan.

With rebored bullet holes
in the innerspring mattresses
of the Rough Rider Hotel,
with freeway exits to the instant West,
of instant coffee in a plastic cup,

he made a town to fit
the picture postcards,
more glittering than the ancient
scoria hills behind it,
and he saw that it was good.

LOYAL CITIZEN

Last week a new dentist
worked on my teeth.
"All of your molars," he said,
"are decayed, awaiting my hand."
It was not what I expected.
He did his work swiftly.

Since then I have no control
over what I say.
My speaking has become
all public pronouncement.
I am wired to the ministry
of purple propaganda.
I give official communiques
continuously.
I believe it is something in the silver.
Always, uninterruptedly,
I am a loyal citizen.
Activated by the hinge in my jaw,
the words come out of my mouth,
stinging my tongue in passing
that cannot measure their morphemes.
My mind, people tell me now,
is predictable,
believing they hear my thinking.
They do not know
they hear nothing of me,
and I cannot tell them.

I have decided to write this now,
in spite of the pain,
as I wait here patiently
in the doctor's office.
He has promised to look at my hand.

TOM McKEOWN *was born in Evanston, Illionis, in 1937. He has taught at various colleges in Michigan, Wisconsin, and Missouri, and his poems have been published in* The New Yorker, *the* Atlantic Monthly, Harper's, Saturday Review, The Nation, Commonweal, *and the* Harvard Advocate. *His first book,* The Luminous Revolver, *was published by Sumac Press.*

THE GRAVEYARD ROAD

The brightest morning of summer,
wind blowing the leaves greener
than imagined, the lake swaying
impossibly toward the sun.

A blonde girl walks down
the graveyard road, barefoot,
ragged in her denims. Her hair
is knotted in a bun, her eyes
are radiant, reaching out.

The dead do not turn in their dark,
do not rise up, do not flow
from the grass. There is stillness
in their cool dust, like the fine
ashes of a distant planet. Part
of her is slowly turning toward
another world that no one knows.

The girl walks on, far from all
the dead or so she thinks. She pulls
a Queen Anne's lace and dreams
she sees the roots breaking stone
in their slow descent.

She looks down at her tan, thin legs,
her ample breasts; her vision of love
warms even the shaded graves.

She runs up the road, feels at that
moment, her running could unshackle
the dead, could swell her room
with yellow flowers. She thinks
this morning her eyes might flatten out
the waves, might make the lake her mirror,
a way to pass through herself and out.

The road is hot, the pebbles bite her feet.
She reaches up, loosens the ribbon about
her hair, and shakes her head, the loveliness
of her gold rains down.

NOVEMBER ON LAKE MICHIGAN

near Pentwater

On the hills behind the dunes,
mottled yellow leaves, pink leaves
running to red, brown leaves blackening.

I think of the storm of November 11, 1940,
the ships breaking up, sixty foot waves,
bodies bloating on the beach, splinters
of wood, islands of grain washing back
and forth in the shallows.

I look at my hands, weak hands and know
that I can change nothing, not the past,
nor the thin minutes of this hour.

The black waves crest, break like whips
that have escaped their masters.

The wind has fallen in love with itself
and will listen to no one.

ROBERT L. McROBERTS *was born in Janesville, Wisconsin, in* 1944. *He graduated from the University of Wisconsin–Oshkosh, earned an M.F.A. at the University of Iowa, and taught at the University of Wisconsin–Superior. He is presently teaching in the creative writing program at Roger Williams College, in Bristol, Rhode Island. His poems have been published in* Arts in Society, Epoch, Choice, Poetry Northwest, Iowa Review, Shenandoah, Quarry, *and other magazines.*

PHOTO OF A RETIRED FARMER, BIG BEND, WISCONSIN

If it is spring, an early warm spring,
and his face is stitched like the quilts
of his jacket, what do the people
at Farm and Fleet know? If his fingers
are so broad that they resemble
the red slats in the snow fence, who
keeps the sheep in?

Wherever he walks, he stoops
to pick up a stick. When he
runs it in a line in the dirt,
he says a few words about spring plowing.
When he flicks it toward the sky,
he is switching the stars
back to the barn.

POEM FOR MY STUDENTS

If I were a rich man, I'd pay
for the privilege of teaching.
RANDALL JARRELL

And yet this is a poem
against you. I have been
warned: familiarity breeds
contempt. So I tell you
to write a paper about apathy.
Write a paper about apathy 500 words long.

Each day my voice
changes. Today there is a new pitch. I will not tell
you to write a paper about apathy; today I will write myself.
I begin with a soft
shoe on the table top.
I write *applause*
on the greenboard. You
applaud. By now
you know that this is mime.
I stand with my mouth
in my pocket.
Do you read me?
I open myself like a book
and begin to tear out pages.
My tie first.
I give you all my ties.
The only sport coat I own.
Onto the pile, my shirt,
ironed only on the front. Shoes, socks. The floor
is cold, I start to shiver, then get mad and reverse
the film.

Listen, do not
use metaphors
or figurative
language, it can
only hurt you.

MARCIA LEE MASTERS, *born in 1917, is the daughter of Edgar Lee Masters. Her first volume of poems,* Intent on Earth, *was published in 1965 by Candlelight Press. In 1970 she was co-winner of the Di Castagnola Award from the Poetry Society of America for her second book of poems in progress, and she has received the poetry awards of both the Society of Midland Authors and the Friends of Literature. Marcia Lee Masters is poetry editor of the* Chicago Tribune Magazine.

THE MAN, MY FATHER

Whether you strode from court to court,
Biting the streets off with opinioned feet,
Or climbed the hills — the land was in your blood:
Your boyhood farm where all men worked, and made
The green come up, the seasons sing.

You knew all skies — all weather — you had known
Since youth when you toiled in the prairie heat;
You knew the warmth of hayfields steaming when
The sun arose and drove like golden bees
Into the mist; you knew the smell of soil
New-crumbled, waiting for the seed; you loved
The juice of things hard-earned like your first books.

No matter where you walked — that early farm
Was in your step, your glance; and when you talked —
The pungent sound of cornfields, and the long
Terse-drying winds swirled up from turgid wheat
Were in your words; even your silences
Had sinew — like tree roots.

Yet, when you lolled, it was with gusto — in
A chair that needed paint, no cushion at
Your back; your feet thrust in the grass, your boots

Still wet from hikes through morning fields, while books
Rose at your side, soon to be husked like corn.

You wrote while others slept, while flowers
Faded in vases, and the rooms grew cold;
The papers mounted: pencils grown too short
To use were cast aside like bits of kindling
Snapped to pieces on a roaring fire.
You had no sympathy for blights that spread
Unchecked, for idle orchards left to crows;
You sprayed potato plants until the bugs
Fell to their death like words knocked from a line.

Something American — bred in the cattle's strength,
The roosters' battles by the road,
Something that gathered substance from the trees —
Was in your spirit's force, your body's pride.

THE HOUSE IN CHICAGO

Mostly, I remember all the books,
And statues, the one of Powys —
Culling the light above the centuries of shelves;
And how the sun, pushing through velvet draperies,
Made little amber forests on the rugs.

The hearth was broad and oaken, one to pace by;
Logs blew up sudden storms of praise;
The porch, designed for scope,
Sat up high to see the winter sunset
Smouldering like some far-sounding battlefield
Whose cannons smoked immortal gold.

And it was in that house,
Beneath an old bright-fruited lamp,

Inlaid with plums and pears,
Congealed forever in a juiceless harvest,
That you read your poems.

Night after night, I heard them;
And they stung me —
As if some great imported traveller
Had scared up all the dust upon a country road.

FIGURE

Night after summer night the drift of pipe-talk reached us,
Around the turning of the country stair:
Stories of graves, and ghosts, and vanishings;
The mistried and pathetic lives of men;
The knots of fate —
The things that choked them; —

Grand intent
Shriveled to a quince.

Yet, when the fancy struck you —
You would tell us of the Grinderpuss,
The wicked bear who hid out in the woods,
And chewed your toe,
Or crowned your head with honeypots.

But, mostly I remember you
Standing upon a hill alone when sunset
Glowed through the clouds
Like a bright-stepped Acropolis;

Your arms locked beyond all words.

JOHN MATTHIAS *was born in Columbus, Ohio, in 1941.
He has published two volumes of poems,* Bucyrus *and* Turns, *with
the Swallow Press, and is editor of the anthology* 23 Modern
British Poets. *He teaches English at the University of Notre Dame.*

ON LAKE MICHIGAN — 1972
(Sinai, Biafra, Pakistan)

Twenty degrees below the normal for May,
    a heavy mist and fierce wind off the lake:
I cut up logs for the iron pot-bellied stove.
    We came here thinking *enough, enough*
(Of Winter & its deaths), and now my daughters
    both are ill, sweating out their fevers
In their sleeping bags . . .

For days they've complained of the smell:
    Alewives in thousands wash up nightly
On the beach. Early every morning I've buried
    these small, grey fish in piles, clearing
The distance for games . . . graves everywhere, mounds,
    holding my nose. Doing that, I easily
Forgot those others digging too, though they were not
    nearby. . . . And digging

Not in campgrounds, but in towns; not on private beaches
    but on beach heads; and not to bury Alewives
But to bury wives — husbands, daughters, sons —
    under the sand, under the earth with
Them all. . . . Even now, kindling wood to keep
    sick children warm, making awkward
Hands do unfamiliar things a hundred miles from
    a telephone or car, I can easily forget
Enough to think I bring on Spring instead of fire.

PETER MICHELSON *was born in Chicago, Illinois, in 1935, and raised in Seattle, Washington. Since 1957 he has lived in Wyoming, North Dakota, Indiana, and Chicago, and he teaches now at the University of Colorado. He is the author of* The Aesthetics of Pornography *(1971) and* The Eater *(1972), and his work has appeared in a wide variety of magazines — from* Oink *to* The New Republic.

WHEN THE REVOLUTION REALLY

comes it will come
   in the dead of winter, while

      you're walking
      down Clark Street
   to the Cosmopolitan State Bank.

   The wind will
   knock an old man
butt over teakettle, his

      cane and shopping bag
   go sprawling. You
         stop and help him up.

      You take his arm.
He will prefer
      to carry the shopping bag

         himself. You
   will walk with him
three blocks to his apartment house. He

will fumble with his keys. He
will mumble that
        he can make it now. It

    will not occur to him
        to thank you.
    Then you will go home rather

    than to the bank, because
you should conduct only so much business
        in a single day.

    Or maybe it will come
in a bus in the Loop
        in August

    a steaming August afternoon, and
    an old lady, really old
        with a cane

    and a shopping bag, mumbling
    to herself like
old ladies do, an

    old lady will announce
    like old ladies do that
        she wants off at Randolph, and

    she'll get up creaky
        and slow, very slow, and
    she'll take a long long time

        getting off:
put the cane on the first step
        take careful hold

of the rail, put
her right foot on
the first step, slowly

twisting her
ponderous old body, then
the other foot on the step, the

cane, then,
on the second step
shift her grip

right foot, body turning, left foot,
and the same thing
all over again

to the ground.
And the bus driver waits
very patiently and

we all sit very
patiently and
we will say, and

we will mean it, that
there's an old lady
getting off the bus, she

goes very slowly
because she's old
and it's hot and

she's tired and
anyway she's not in a hurry.
Neither are we. We're

just sitting here
and it's all right. That's
the way old ladies do.

Then you'll know
the revolution
has really happened.

PARABLE FOR OUR TIME

A little bird whispers in their ear
and, inexplicably, the city hires
freaks and bums.
Music, dancing, jugglers, clowns, poets
carrying on at the city center.
Pretty soon people start hanging out there,
eating their lunch,
singing and dancing and carrying on,
climbing on the Picasso,
which is all right
because the engineers figure out
how many cubic inches of people
can fit on cubic inches of the Picasso
and they build it strong enough.
But there's a cop who doesn't know that
and he figures it's not OK
so he goes to tell everyone to get off.
Meanwhile, there's this girl who,
either as a tactical freak ploy
or maybe she always wanted to diddle a cop,
anyway she seduces him
before he tells everyone to get off,
so they hump happily in the shade of the Picasso
while everyone is singing and dancing and carrying on.
After while everybody goes home or back to work,

just sort of boppin along
bop bop bop . . .
The cop, who is so pleased he
forgets to mess anybody over,
goes home and tells his wife he got laid,
in the line of duty,
keeping the peace.
She says, *what!?*
He says he got laid.
So his wife says, *how was she?*
He says, *what!?*
How was she?
The cop is speechless.
So his wife says, *never mind, I'm better,*
and anyway you don't need to go to work to get laid.
So they put the kids to bed
and then they go to bed,
and sure enough, *she's better!*
He never noticed.
So the next day he doesn't go to work.
He stays home and gets laid.
And the people are all getting together
at the center of the city, carrying on.
Singing, dancing, talking, laughing.
Climbing on the Picasso.
Each day the cop stays home and gets laid.
But he forgets to tell them down at the cop station,
so they keep sending him his check
because there's never any trouble on his beat.
And the Picasso is strong enough.
Even the bosses come down for the party.
The rest of the city is just like before,
but down at the center everything is fine.
Singing and dancing. Carrying on.
The city gives the cop a raise.
Everyone agrees he's earned it.

RALPH J. MILLS, JR., *was born in Chicago, Illinois, in 1931, attended Lake Forest College, and received a Ph.D. at Northwestern University. He has taught at the University of Chicago, and is presently a professor of English at the University of Illinois at Chicago Circle. His recent books include an edition of poet David Ignatow's* Notebooks *(Swallow Press), a volume of critical essays on recent American poetry,* Cry of the Human *(University of Illinois Press), and a collection of poems,* Door to the Sun *(Baleen Press).*

THE WHITE PIANO

> *the sleeping water of pianos*
> RAFAEL ALBERTI

Sunlight inches down
the leaded panes of an alcove

Dust drowns a sleeping keyboard,
hammers anchored to silence
wash in an odor of wood, green felt,
the tide of dead hours

No one's here
Wind and the day flown up the chimney

But I listen for the play of fingers
gone into stone and grass,
my ear bent to catch chords like lost breath

Small white piano,
cold air and oblivion —
a thread of remembrance still spools the years

Tonight from another window
I watch the moon
floating in its circle of borrowed light

DOOR TO THE SUN
for Kenneth Becker, d. 1972

Clouds swollen with rain
like a purple bruise

In the yard of a deserted house
blue wildflowers wink tiny petalled eyes
among weeds and branches
the only light left under gaping windows

You have died
I hear weeks after
to think of our talks
and the shape of your hand

Something slips away with you
back over trees and water
through grains and leaf skeletons
where the last drops suddenly glow

In one of your paintings
a northern forest and lake
burn up into yellow sky
as if the black bones of pines falling
touched a door to the sun

JUDITH MINTY, *born in 1937, lives in North Muskegon, Michigan, with her husband and three children in a house with many animals. She is presently doing translations, writing fiction, and completing her second volume of poetry. Her first book,* Lake Songs and Other Fears, *was the 1973 recipient of the United States Award of the International Poetry Forum, in Pittsburgh, Pennsylvania. Her poems have appeared in the* Atlantic Monthly, Poetry Northwest, New York Quarterly, Poetry, *and* Green River Review.

FINDING ROOTS

She is a weak sister, that ocean.
I have wasted my life
searching for kin, looking for blood
along slashes of highway. Roots

should spring from the land, I thought,
and so dug, but always reached oceans.
Scavenged the beaches, sifted
through spindrift on salt-water shores,

put shells to my ear, heard
echoes, but never my name,
found bones of coral, fossils
that bore no family ties.

And so finished by turning
inland, ebbed back to the source
away from salt, from parents
of waves that lick hardest at wounds,

to the spring of beginnings.
Found plants that hold
hard to the soil, North,
where ice melts slowly from glaciers.

BOUNDARIES

The call of the old cock pheasant breaks
into morning. He struts the line
that marks my land from his and I
stand my ground. With hooded eyes,
we dare each other to cross over.

When we beat our wings against years
a harsh cry rises in the throat. I hear
him again. He wants the brown hen.
Before dusk she must watch him
ruffle his feathers under the juniper bush.

THE END OF SUMMER

1

The old bitch labrador swims
in heavy circles. Under water
her legs run free without their limp.
She stretches brown eyes toward me,
snorting water, and the stick I throw
stirs gray memories of ten Octobers,
ducks that fly at the sun and fall.

2

On the Pere Marquette River, salmon
quiver upstream from the lake: a return
to alpha. At the dam
they leap and throw themselves
through currents, stretch
and spend themselves against the torrent
from the falls, lie torn on rocks.

3

All week the sky has been filled
with orange petals. Monarch butterflies
floating in cycles toward milkweed.
Freed from their jade chrysalis,
they have been waiting for the wind's
current to die. The beach
is covered with torn wings.

4

The merganser carries fire
on his hood. All summer
he has nested in our channel, drifted
with the half-tame mallards. His sharp bill
stabs the water to catch bread I throw.
He belongs by the sea. I want him
to fly now before October and guns.

G . E . M U R R A Y , *born in* 1945, *was educated at Canisius College and Northeastern and Brown universities. His first book of poems was* A Mile Called Timothy *(Ironwood Press,* 1972*); a second collection,* Holding Fast, *was published by Brown University Press in* 1974. *In* 1973 *he received a Bridgeman Scholarship from the Bread Loaf Writers' Conference. Murray, a contributing editor to* Fiction International, *lives in Oak Park, Illinois.*

THE DRIVING WHEELS

> *I feel like some old engine
> that's lost its driving wheel.*
>
> AS SUNG BY TOM RUSH

I am thinking of Iowa
After Christmas in a roadhouse,

The wind's force, and coffee
Like a driving wheel.

Don't take coffee lightly.
It's a nation builder!

The holy aroma of work
Is ground-roasted & bitter, too.

A sprocket for our driving wheels?
The darker the better, eh?

The wind, like coffee, warms
Our smiles. The wind is everything.

Looking across the breast
Plate of pickle-green Iowa,

I think over the clack
Of saucers, & wet napkins

Soaking our spills —
A tonic for the smudges

Of Christmas. It is morning
In Des Moines, & still no snow.

"Pass the cream, please . . ."
I feel dark natives

Shucking pods & grinning
Like the smooth, fat blades

Of machetes. Quick as weeds,
The wind pockets our lives,

Our crashing cups & anger.
Outside, the highway sags.

Corn steams in Iowa
Like a day-old pot,

A barnful of *National Geographics*,
A faith in brown beans.

I heal from a flow of coffee
Cut fresh from my throat,

Swell through the ruins
Of a terrible distance.

These wheels . . .

THE PLANT RHYTHMS

I know the tops of shoes now, stalking out to land's end.
The brush of a client's walk, the squeeze and shine of
packaged feet . . . a skin on skin! . . . I am the earth within, a
beat quicker than stone or agent. I hear dry sticks crack, and
lie alone, like lost arrows . . . My tissues touch the edge of
old, curious injuries: something small and distant — a bullet
or lighthouse — that comes like a puncture: manicured grass
on-file, plaster models, catalogs, the useless sale of space! . . .

But space returns to itself with deaths — clear, senseless,
the same . . . And I thrive: a huge, deep sound in myself,
like the shoreline gaining among smoke and sea. I bless the
faint twitch of insects; their nervous legs humming a mad
performance, a string movement. Then only the delicate and
deaf spring to the rhythms of what I am.

A PAVEMENT ARTIST

I have changed nothing but coins.
From a stretch in the heart,
I hunch by the same shop front
Working my stubs of chalk
Into tiny, cement arguments
With blue ducks, passers-by
And oaks mislaid in motion.

For a moment they are mine.
And I am a goat drunk
With wild chives, art and garbage.
An insulting hawk with pastel
Claws in my trousers —
The light animal.
But cement collects scraps of the flesh;
There are no ridges left in my thumbs.
Even the windows I touch
Stay clear and printless.
Is it raining? Are the ducks
Diving beneath their blue coats?
A duck can't swim
In this awkward, wet powder.
My hands are paste again.
I can change nothing but coins.

LINDA PARKER-SILVERMAN *was born in Oak Park, Illinois, in* 1942. *She attended Northwestern University and the University of Michigan. In* 1972 *she won a first prize, major award for poetry, in the Hopwood competition, and she has published her work in* Chelsea *and other magazines. She lives on a farm in Ypsilanti, Michigan.*

NURSING HOME

she cannot see
them rolling her morning
opiates through the pastel doors

they change her water
and ask her how her heart
carries its years

thick with flowers
thick with flowers
she replies

they wheel her
away from the shapes
moving behind the windows

the forms
that have begun to
stroke her temples

but at night
she hears the animal
that wears roots around

its neck
coming to tear apart
the blossoms

ADVICE TO THE LOVELORN

They are aging in attic
beds that have no pelts
and drink from goblets
that are oxidizing:

there are ten thousand
beds in the dark
that are not beds,
where no animal bones
lift the sheets.

I have a house
that breaks into flowers
when my old animal
comes back to spread
himself across my skin.

He is a sheep fur,
white and curled;
even in sleep his eyes
are my road lights
through night country.

MARK PERLBERG, *born in* 1929, *lives with his family in Chicago, Illinois, where he works as an editor. He is the author of* The Burning Field *(William Morrow,* 1970)*, and his poems have appeared in* Hudson Review, The New Yorker, *the* Atlantic Monthly, Chicago Review, *and other publications.*

WATER AND LIGHT, LIGHT AND WATER

1

At the lake's edge
In an inch of water
Minnows move above sand ridges
Stroked by loops, by nets of light.

2

The late sun hangs over the lake's rim.
Rings of light, shaken from the water
Climb the cedars.
Along the broken pier the clear light
Sings in the thistles.

IN PRAISE OF LICHEN

It lives on mere banks and drifts of air
And where nothing else will,
Growing in ashy moonbursts on bare boulders
   in the sun's brightest flare, beneath a shine of ice,
   in blowing salt air.
Its medallions color the bark of trees;
They seal gravestones — a glad sign
In the windy margins of the world, of increase
Near the domain of zero.

STANLEY PLUMLY *was born in* 1939. *He is currently a visiting lecturer at the University of Iowa's Writers' Workshop and an editor for the* Ohio Review. *He has published two books of poems,* In the Outer Dark *and* Giraffe *(Louisiana State University Press). Plumly was awarded a Guggenheim grant in poetry in 1973, and won the Delmore Schwartz Memorial Award, for his first book of poems.* ["One Song" is dedicated to his father.]

PORCHES

In southeastern Ohio there are porches,
one to a hill, that lean into the calm
like the decks of ships too long, too far out.
The coal is gone and the children have nothing to say.
And in the leftover towns the men fall asleep in their hands.
And the women stand on the porches in the evening
inside the deep eye of the sun,
listening for some kind of wind,
fixed utterly in any direction.

ONE SONG

I want the grave to be six by six
so I can stand you up,
arms lifted like a tree,
and watch you grow back
into the world, back into me.

I want to plant you like the vertical dead,
both hands kneaded into fists in air,
then I want your hands to open
like deep flowers once the wind,
like breath, is rain and sun

(and open, I want them to rise
to a full arm's length of bone,
the whole body flowering out of them,
until they hold the ground together
where ground was broken).

I want to get you deep enough to go
down, down beyond the mind
in death, too close to the carnal quick
of being alive and thinking this.
I want to bury bones to where they bend, not break.

PULL OF THE EARTH

A man lies down to sleep,
to let go of the day,
and however he turns,
whatever his body believes,

he feels the earth fall away
and the eye, even in dream,
follow the perfect curve,
and though for the while

the dream may let him go,
still the day comes back
each infinitely slow step
of the way from dark.

And if in sleep I sometimes
reach for you, across
whatever distances
we dream, across the distance

I am dreaming now,
against silence
and the body's fear of falling,
if I reach across this space —

barely the width of one of us —
and you turn to me,
your full face pale
and perfect as a moon,

dream or real, as the blind
know braille, I follow
that face, its body,
and hold what I can.

FELIX POLLAK *was born in Vienna, Austria, in 1909, and came to the United States as a refugee from Hitler in 1938. He has a doctor of jurisprudence degree from the University of Vienna and an M.A. in library science from the University of Michigan. He was, until his retirement, the curator of rare books and "little magazines" at the University of Wisconsin in Madison, and is poetry editor of* Arts in Society. *Pollak has published three books of poems, the latest being* Ginkgo (Elizabeth Press).

NOFRETETE

She is Queen Nofretete translated into
Walgreen's. See
the regal cheekbones guarding
amygdaloid eyes, see
these *l'inconnue de la Nile* lips luminate
under the blue neon as under an alien moon, see
the chiseled knuckles scoop
scoops of ice cream into paper cups . . . oh it pangs me
to hear her say, chocolate or vanilla mister . . . !

HISTORICAL SOCIETY EXHIBIT: OLD PROGRAMME

Glance at this fabled page straight from
the fairy book of fame, framed black against
a gilded wall, and read a footnote:
    Miss Beverly Poole
is ill and her role will be played by Miss Ives
tonight. Tears under glass, still wet.
    (What flurry, what
intrigue?) Can a skeleton tell of a
woman's breasts and the shape of her lips?
    Can the sweet

bread of time be sliced and kept under glass,
    unchanging
proclaiming a change? Poor Beverly.
And Dorothea? Was it the trampoline swing into
the high winds for her? (Fame dies when
questioned.) The mute light
    refracting yellow on the glass
Beverly's malady, Dorothea's health,
both cured now.

HOW I GOT MYSELF TRAPPED

for Philip Dacey

It was easy.
I took one right step
after another.

CARL RAKOSI, *born in* 1903, *lives in Minneapolis, Minnesota. He retired in* 1968, *having worked mainly as a psychotherapist and social worker. His most recent book of verse is* Ere-Voice, *and he has had work in* The Nation, Chelsea, Quarterly Review of Literature, Massachusetts Review, Midstream, *and* Iowa Review.

THE COUNTRY SINGER

There ain't nothin special about me.
Everybody knows I'm too fat
and my legs are too short.
I'm just a middle-aged cornball
with a loud voice
and a drinking problem.
It's a funny thing,
when I'm on stage
all I do is act like me.
But I can act me
like a son of a bitch!

THE OLD CODGER'S LAMENT

Who can say now,
'When I was young, the country was very beautiful?
Oaks and willows grew along the rivers
and there were many herbs and flowering bushes.
The forests were so dense the deer slipped through
the cottonwoods and maples unseen.'

Who would listen?
Who will carry even the vicarious tone of that time?

In the old days
        age was honored.
Today it's whim,
        the whelp without habitat.

Who will now admit
        that he is either old or young
or knows anything?
All that went out with the forests.

DAVID RAY, *born in Sapulpa, Oklahoma, in 1932, has published four collections of poems:* X-Rays, Dragging the Main, A Hill in Oklahoma, *and* Gathering Firewood. *Recent poems of his have appeared in* American Review, American Poetry Review, *and elsewhere. In 1971 he founded the quarterly* New Letters *at the University of Missouri-Kansas City.*

STOPPING NEAR HIGHWAY 80

We are not going to steal the water tower
in Malcom, Iowa,
just stop for a picnic right under it.
Nor need they have removed the lightbulb
in the city park
nor locked the toilet doors.
We are at peace, just eating and drinking
our *poco vino* in Malcom, Iowa,
which evidently once had a band
to go with its bandstand.
We walk down the street, wondering how
it must be to live behind the shades
in Malcom, Iowa, to peer out,
to remember the town as it was before
the Expressway discovered
it, subtracted what would flow
on its river eastwards and westwards.
We are at peace, but when we go into the bar
in Malcom, Iowa, we find that the aunts
and uncles drinking beer have become
monsters and want to hurt us and we do
not know how they could have ever
taken out the giant breasts
of childhood or cooked the fine biscuits
or lifted us up high on the table
or have told us anything at all
we'd ever want to know
for living lives as gentle as we can.

RAVENNA

And what did we see, high up there
in mosaics
but the old cousins, Beatrice, Edris, Alice
holding cups of gold, their haloes
awkward like the strawhats
they wore in the beanfields

THE BLUE DUCK

An idea can be glazed, captured, brought down
From heaven!
Our feathers can become blue,
Even a beak can smile!
This duck crouches in a world that cannot
Break it, says Open our eyes,
Let them become luminous,
Amused, and kind!
Duck says to so much: I am not interested.
Duck says Let us feel this blue floating
Down from heaven, let us have thoughts
Between us, let us be fearless.
Duck says Consider the dumbness of animals,
How wonderful it is not to care about death,
To go on falling away from this worst nature
That has been patted upon us like clay.
Duck says we can sit still and go on swimming
Toward the infinite.
Duck says we do not have to judge
With pleasure or displeasure or tell
Ourselves it is all for the best or not.
Duck shows us how naked he is,
How obscene it is to wear a helmet.
Duck says, even to Sunday crowds,
We are lovers, we are without purpose!

J A M E S   R E I S S , *born in 1941, grew up in New York City. He attended the University of Chicago where he took two degrees and won two Academy of American Poets' prizes. Since then he has taught English and creative writing at Miami University (Ohio). He and his wife recorded and edited* Self-Interviews by James Dickey *(Doubleday, 1970), and his first book of poems,* The Breathers, *was published by the Ecco Press (Viking) in 1974. His poems have appeared in such places as* Antioch Review, The New Yorker, *and* The New Republic, *and he is the regular poetry critic for the* Cleveland Plain Dealer.

THE BREATHERS

(Jeffrey Andrew Reiss — October 5, 1969)

In Ohio, where these things happen,
we had been loving all winter.
By June you looked down and saw your belly
was soft as fresh bread.

In Florida, standing on the bathroom
scales, you were convinced —
and looked both ways for a full minute before crossing
Brickell Boulevard.

In Colorado you waited-out summer in a mountain
cabin, with Dr. Spock,
your stamps, and my poems in the faint
8000-foot air.

Listen, he had a perfect body,
right down to his testicles, which I counted.
The morning he dropped from your womb, all rosy
as an apple in season, breathing the thick
fall air of Ohio, we thought good things would happen.

Believe me, Dr. Salter and the nurses were right:
he was small but feisty — they said he was
feisty. That afternoon in his respirator
when he urinated it was something to be proud of.
Cyanotic by evening, he looked like a dark rose.

Late that night you hear . . .

Think of the only possible twentieth century consolations:
Doris saying it might have been better this way;
think of brain damage, car crashes, dead soldiers:
better seventeen hours than eighteen, twenty years
or half-life in Ohio where nothing happens.

Late that night you hear them
in the . . .

For, after all, we are young, traveling
at full speed into the bull's eye of the atom.
There's a Pepsi and hot dog stand in that bull's eye,
and babies of the future dancing around us.
Listen, the air is thick with our cries!

Late that night you hear them
in the nursery, the breathers.
Their tiny lungs go in and out like the air
bladder on an oxygen tank
or the rhythm of sex.
Asleep, your arms shoot towards that target
with a stretch that lifts you like a zombie,
wakes you to the deafening breathers.
And now you see them, crawling
rings around your bed, in blankets,
buntings, preemies in incubators circling
on casters, a few with cleft palates, heart trouble,
all feistily breathing, crawling
away from your rigidly outstretched arms —
breathing, robbing the air.

JOHN CALVIN REZMERSKI *was born in* 1942. *His work has appeared in* South Dakota Review, New Letters, Chelsea, *and numerous other magazines, and a collection of his poems,* Held for Questioning, *was published by the University of Missouri Press in* 1969. *He teaches at Gustavus Adolphus College in Saint Peter, Minnesota.*

SOME GOOD THINGS LEFT AFTER THE WAR
WITH THE SIOUX

My eyes welcome high grass,
green going yellow
shooting up
from old old earth
fed with hard-earned blood
and bled sweat.
This soil now marked by tractor tires
fed Amos Huggins in 1862
and feeds me now,
feeds you,
and the blood it has swallowed
never spoils the corn.
It is the magic of that blood,
red cells and white cells,
and clear yellow fluid
falling on the warm black earth
that keeps legs pumping
up the valley and over the bluffs
to mourn the innocent,
to cherish the giving,
to pray with fast breath
to the breath of the land,
nitrogen rising
from remains of quiet and boastful alike,
seeping into the roots of rosebushes,
the strength of wheat,

the warmth of beans,
the sweetness of corn and pork,
the plumpness of lovers,
into children of grass and grain
and the spirit of the blood,
hundred-proof blood,
drunk-making blood,
man-making blood,
blood contaminated only by blood,
into the children of the eye,
of the spleen,
of the brain and the voice,
into the welcomers of grass,
welcomers of dawn
on the blue and brown earth,
welcomers of silence
and forgivers of fire and the plow and old murders.

PETTIGREW MUSEUM

Somewhere in all this mess,
things stacked up in cases
and outside of cases
upstairs or downstairs,
I expect to find
Sitting Bull
preserved
in all his feathers, beads,
dentalium shells,
elkskin suit,
quill-embroidered,
buried under all the hatchets,
all the quartzite pipes,
sinew-stitched moccasins,
Dakota hymnals,
beadwork,

pipe bags.
Somewhere under there.
If I find him, I'll know
buried even farther down
minus his scalp
minus his bad arm
Little Crow is still trying
to tell us to go home.

DRIVING AT NIGHT

The radio brings whole cities
into my head.
Philadelphia, Kansas City,
Houston,
Louisville,
St. Louis, Minneapolis.
They fly in at me
out of the dark
full of people talking, dying,
committing crimes.
They are at war,
blasting each other with static,
pushing each other aside
in the air
as though my head
is the last safe place
for a city to be.

MICHAEL RYAN *was born in Saint Louis, Missouri, in 1946. His poems have appeared in* Poetry, The New Yorker, Poetry Northwest, The Nation, *and many other magazines. His first book,* Threats Instead of Trees, *was the winner of the Yale Series Of Younger Poets competition for 1973. He has taught in the Writers' Workshop at the University of Iowa, and served as poetry editor for* Iowa Review.

HITTING FUNGOES

Hitting fungoes to a bunch
of kids who asked me
nicely, I'm afraid the hard
ball they gave me might
shatter the stained-glass
window of the church
across this abandoned lot.
I see it all now, in
the moment the ball leaves
my hand before it smacks
the bat: we scatter
in every possible direction
but the pastor, sensing
a pervert, screams
to the cops to chase
the big one, and there
I am: trapped. I pull
my old Woodrow Wilson
Fellowship Letter out
of my worn suit pocket,
swing it wildly, but they
smell last night's sex
on my breath, condemn
me to jail for failure
to forget old needs or failure
itself. I swing without

thinking, the only way,
and the crack is the scream
of a hip-bone ripped
from its socket
on the rack. Not bad.
Not too deep, but a nice
arching loft. One kid,
who runs faster than the others,
makes a spectacular
diving catch & throws it back.

YOUR OWN IMAGE

When by mistake you miss
the urinal in a public place,
there's no bending down, cleaning
up, or betting others won't
step in it. So you zip
your zipper with a flourish,
hoping the guy in the nearest
stall is admiring your follow
through & not the spreading puddle
which at least is your very own.
You stroll casually to the wash-
stand, avoiding thoughts
of barefoot little kids & cripples
whose leather laces brush
the floor and the curious eyes
that compare you to Pontius Pilate
as you wash your hands,
but you can't help meeting
your own image as you finish
the ablutions. It says,
You are dark and handsome.

ERNEST SANDEEN *was born in Warren County, Illinois, in 1908, and is presently a professor of English at the University of Notre Dame.* Poems *of his have appeared in* Poetry, Minnesota Review, Iowa Review, The New Yorker, Saturday Review, Poetry Northwest, Sewanee Review, Hudson Review, *and elsewhere. His second volume of poems,* Children and Older Strangers, *was published in 1962.*

MAIL FROM HOME IN THE SKY

Cozy above us a little airplane chugs
along, all in white. It feels like a pet bird
that knows its home, a throb of our neighborhood
warm in the sky.

              We watch it turn to slow
pastel pink, surprised yet not surprised.
(Have we, then, begun to remember?) Its toy
motor stills, only our blood thumps the air.

It curves its homespun wings, it's looking
down for a place to fall to and be sick in,
decides with a sudden dip and plunges.
Listening for the crash we grow back down
to children, smaller, smaller, hands pressed hard
but not too hard against ears. When it sounds,
the crash is fur and cotton, we have to hunt
it down past corners limp as water, our legs
are as young as fins.

                            And Mr. D'Arcy's roof
is not caved in, the Hornbacks' garden is not
in ruins. The wreckage lies content among
junked cars in Mr. Garcia's lot next
to the tracks. Fuselage, wings and tail
have crumbled off like sunset, only the tiny
motor grins, intact and dead.

No flame or smoke. The pilot's body has slid
down the smell of hot oil and grease to nothing.
Policemen dressed as important people are poking
looks like x-rays at everything and everybody.
But what can *they* do? Indoors at home we know
that what has happened can't unhappen, ever.

HOWARD SCHWARTZ *was born in Saint Louis, Missouri, in 1945, and continues to live there. He is a graduate of Washington University, and in 1969 received the first place award in the Academy of American Poets poetry contest held there. Since 1970 he has taught poetry and short story writing courses at the University of Missouri in Saint Louis. His first book,* A Blessing over Ashes, *was published in 1974 by Tree Books, and his work has appeared in approximately seventy-five magazines, including* Chicago Review, Minnesota Review, *and* New York Quarterly.

MAPS

At night all the maps grow blank
First the rocks wear away
The footholds
The warpaths
Each and every sacred pool
Trees are uprooted
Fields ready for harvest
One by one
Every province is eclipsed

All the while
Snow can be seen
Stealing roses from mounds
Memories from cold stone
Carrying off the last lake
Between two mountains
Slowly the raised outlines
Shift with the shades of gray
That filter through the dark
Slowly one beach imposes itself
On every other
One tide returns crest above crest

When all the oceans are uncharted
The earth is a glowing coal
Lost in space
Seen from a distance
The planet inscribes
A circle
Burning into a blank page
No more than the outline
Of an eclipse.

CONTAINMENT

> Anyone can create a bamboo garden in the world, but who
> can incorporate the world into his bamboo grove?
>
> HERMANN HESSE

When the world has lost
Another sun

And I cannot contain
The darkness
Before it spills inside,

Each simple shoot
Dons the mask
It has concealed,

Each forking path
Pulls further apart,

The boundaries
Of the circle
Cannot find the center,

Waves swell
From unseen roots

And no covenant
Can restrain
The flood.

LOVE POEM

She coils her body around me
Coils one leg
Around my waist
My hands form the soft clay of her body
Search for her center
Give her hands
A home
My mouth pauses at more than one place

Eyes closed
We know nothing of darkness
Of the river that runs through our sleep
Coiled inside
A seashell
The voice of the falls
Sounds our sleep
Until parted from our dreams

Her hands sleep between us
Like warm birds
Share the heat of folded wings
Her nipples ask for nothing more
Than my mouth
The words of my tongue

The earth grows full again
A blossom breaks open
Between us
More than one moon tears free
Untold longing
Illumined from below.

R. E. SEBENTHALL, *born in 1917, lives in Mount Horeb,
Wisconsin. Her first collection of poetry,* Acquainted with a
Chance of Bobcats, *was published by Rutgers University Press in
1970, and her poems have appeared in many magazines, including*
Western Humanities Review, Perspective, Poetry Northwest,
Massachusetts Review, *and* Beloit Poetry Journal.

THE VILLAGES

They have forgotten what wolves
first drove them to huddle
the hard winters of needing each other
the comfort of manyness
under the tall nights of the forest

they could scatter now
each house achieve
a miracle of space and air
but they are clamped
to the iron pipes, the tough cables
of easy fire
instant light and water

worse, they have stared
at themselves too long
across the backyard fence
at the drugstore corner

now the picture windows can't
find anything new to say
the mirrors contain
a community face
the chimneys dispatch
identical letters to heaven

THE OLD ONES

immured in thickening walls
and filming windows,
no longer try to grasp
the shapes and words
flashing past too swiftly outside
like unidentifiable birds;

room by room, the house
gives up; in the parlor
on the claw-foot table
the family album gathers dust
and puzzling faces;

weeds draw closer, the path
to the mailbox fades,
the porch step sags,
the old dog dies;

only the kitchen
is heated now, only
the cellar-cricket
holds off silence.

BRUCE SEVERY, *born in* 1947, *lives with his wife and daughter in North Dakota.* He has published poems in Dacotah Territory, Measure, Café Solo, *and other magazines. His first book of poetry,* Crossing into the Prairies, *was published in* 1974.

TALKS WITH HIMSELF

you have gone through
a hundred rabbit lives,
walked a hundred miles
of noisy shelter belts,
driven every dirt road
in North Dakota,

you have no treasures to show
but spoil banks
of empty shotgun shells,
you own no land,

but sit in a borrowed outhouse
by the new highway
and lay down thoughts
like windrows,

the mosquitos go off
like firecrackers
on the screens
in the climbing heat
of the dawn.

FINALLY

we brought them
morality

and because
they knew better

we brought them
determination
in crates
by helicopter

wasted it on them

were forced to bring them
the moon
a lunar landscape
of victories

we got that for them
finally

and left them
with sucrose and morphine
in throwaway bags
that will drip
into a corpse's ankle even

and yes
they loved us for that
finally.

FRAMES ON BRIGHT FACES

the world is a wind
tearing at the prairies,
take refuge behind
a blizzard of time,
bed down with solitude,
chisel the walls

and whispers
with having lived,
with having left,
narrate our sexes
as they have weathered,
caulk the inlays
with basic metals,
open inner windows,
get quiet inside,
withdraw from the bench mark,
the theory of standards,
dance a dance
of ghosts,
come sooner.

CROSSING INTO THE PRAIRIES

1 *Prelude*

I am an old man
gone sour in the teeth
and thumbs
confined like compost
to the garden of my years
squash and gourds, long-necked, and children
as durable as winter
but gone like crows and teal, green-winged
raised out of me
and I dream the tracking dreams
under barren ash and aspen
the etching tools, the
parings of fingernails
planted at four corners
of the four winds
of the four Dakotas
and the old hound, Tietjens
who howls at night

when the stars look back
howls at the turtle
in the night sky,
the world was old then
and I was running.

2 *The Myth*

the hunter as cartographer:
up Red River of the North
on late ice
from Pipestone
in crocus push
legged across to Thief River Falls
to the diviner's pool
where fingerlings of grief dart
at the call of the shaman snipe,
I built a medicine wheel
with the long spoke
pointing at the pool
and cairned the other stones
water-smooth and oracular
on the frogged bank,
the rocks became rabbits
and ran away,

spared from the sickness of
the man called smallpox
all dust and pus
and teacher of thirst,
I dragged two shadows home,
at village they laughed
at who could but lead himself
who brings not meat but remedies
"You have coots flapping
in your head," they said but
my wife and I left
scattered the tipi ring

broke up the rocks, put out the
fire of our first year,

left for the land
beneath the lake
that bats talk about at night,

the follower stops,

we passed petroglyphs
of family lines, half-cut
death masks
and pictures of the man
smallpox,

we watched possum and buzzard
lose fights with the sun,
my wife became a turtle
and led to the prairie
under her lake of shields
we are now the pebbles
along the shore
and we remember,

imagine: suggestions of ochre
while we rust.

3 *A Beginning*

there is a fire
in my brain
lignite visions of terrible horses
clamoring
in the prairie wind and visions
of being tamed like rain
by a place
in time
if the sod can hold,
the wild noises of sight
in exile
are like oats blown.

MICHAEL SHERIDAN *was born in Fort Madison, Iowa,
in 1943. He taught for two years at a Job Corps center near San
Francisco, several more years on Truk Island in Micronesia, and is
currently teaching at Geneseo (Illinois) High School and completing
work on his M.F.A. degree at the Writers' Workshop at the Univer-
sity of Iowa. His work has appeared in* the American Poetry Re-
view, December, New Letters, *and other magazines, and a chap-
book,* Warm Spell, *is scheduled for publication. He is married and
the father of two daughters.* ["Grace" is dedicated to John
Skoyles.]

GRACE

My family, in Christian pantomime,
ate from a common bowl.
After dinner we said a rosary
for Russia, for mobs
hoisting heads on sticks.

I loved my father & bless
the Ireland he left
with its excess of virgins,
its queers with monsignors' noses.
Holding anything close,
I expected a rival.
I didn't know the fifth season
the crazy stumble into.

Yesterday on the prairie
I saw a closed wound called Bishop Hill:
there, in the 1850s, nutty Jansonists
sold celibacy to marrieds
and, for color, heaped wild flowers
on the bed of their murdered leader,
expecting him to rise
like Christ on the third day.

He didn't budge.
So they buried him on a ridge
overlooking his new Jerusalem,
body very gray & formal.
Today his ghost is small change.

I paid up & drove home,
where my room seemed large with absence.
Later, rain woke me
back to my body in a rush.
I felt like a one-legged man
with an incredible urge to dance.
For a long time I felt like this.

It's noon now of a dark Sunday.
Down the street
the Episcopal bells chime
a little tune for business.
There's mist inside my room,
transparent as grace,
and wind outside
shrinking in the trees.

I'm so hungry
I can taste the dead.

MARY SHUMWAY, *born in 1926, was raised in Wisconsin Dells, Wisconsin. She was educated at the University of Chicago, San Francisco State College, and the University of Denver, and is currently a member of the faculty at the University of Wisconsin–Stevens Point.* Headlands, *her second collection of poetry, was published in 1972, and her work has appeared in such magazines as* Arts in Society, Beloit Poetry Journal, Cimarron Review, Commonweal, Denver Quarterly, *and* New Orleans Review.

FLIGHT

a hound bays in the blood again
though the moon's down

last night the Northerns pulsed
echoed that vast slow heartbeat

of the universe and woke the dog
that courses there; bound, the bane

of sensible cells, that sly old
predator of light. Tonight birches

turn the silver bellies of their leaves
and in the bog a barn burns

with St. Elmo's fire; the hackles
rise blue and a numbing bay begins.

Snout tight to track, his sniffs
have found these heels and

I cannot run nor stay, prey
and hunter, one, when light wheels.

WHETHER FIRELOCKED

silked, or smoked from that field
above the river, native to August
I woke to dark when the skins of sky

dry taut on the poles of the weather,
brought into night when the vents
give a sweetgrass moonlight,

a firefly or two, with neither love
nor paint rising, flint-hooved,
feathered, out of the east; in fact,

before the full and the wintergreen
and the tamaracks' beginning gold,
red shift in some Doppler dance,

and caught in these hills,
a spark or weave or smoked elk craft
of chance.

CATTAILS FOR BENNETT

Novembers, half a stalk high,
we frisked these fields for arrowheads
and shards, chased foxes, raced the wind
for tickle grass, and lost

> would you remember the gold
> of daylight tamaracks, the green
> and yellow squash in clumps of vine
> scattered on the rise

we rested in the vetch and horsetail
gullied just above the Springs

where cattails nodded no to time
and time arrived

      that hill of grass wheated
      by the sun — across the marsh
      beyond the trees — is windrowed now
      where sumac rimmed and roared each fall

now frost takes the light   I should not
have stopped, but east above the Springs
a half moon bronzed the mist (the pond
was glass — obsidian) and shocked

      the stalks of dark along the field
      and though the blades of weather still
      plow up the flakes of stone and stars
      no finds are here

without you, this: time stays

W A R R E N   S L E S I N G E R , *born in* 1933, *was raised in Kansas City, Missouri. He attended the Writers' Workshop at the University of Iowa, and lived for eight years in Wisconsin while he was a salesman, manager, and editor for a textbook publisher. He taught part-time at Olivet College and at the University of Wisconsin–Milwaukee, and at present is an assistant professor of English at the College of Wooster. In* 1970 *he published* Field with Figurations *(Cummington Press).*

PINE NEEDLES

We arrive like sunlight in winter: tentative
and hesitant, since we have forced the season.
The bud born naked to the twig in spring
is squat, as solid as a frozen raisin.

We bless the white resilience of each seed
which resisted the winter with its tight, precise
intensity its strength, and cherish them:
each sweet and latent packet cased in ice.

Our breath is dense and resinous. We came to preach
the gospel in a cold and northern air
where what we say is a wraith of words which glides,
lapses and fades at the end of an empty pier.

Our own thoughts are all we own
at this our solitary testimonial; for we,
whatever we conceive, whether it is formed or shapeless,
are what the scene receives.

The woods are pined and silent. The beach shelves
and shifts as it winds into the shoreline. No matter
the inswept sense of prayer, we are alone
when the wind walks the pent and gloss of the water.

PASSAGE

3:30

an emptiness

in which he rises like an old balloon
to touch the side and glide to freedom from the grey,
the shaken racket of a train; a gap
in which he reawakens is a car as cool and colorless
as water; no other passengers
are present;
                in sleep the face inflates;
a numbness in the hands, the feet; the substance of a dream
in which he sees the speechless teeth, the tongue
suspended for a second; and then, the breath
with its tepid strangeness: the window wet, the forehead
                pressed
upon it white and sightless in a dream;
                                        a car as cool,
as colorless as water; no other passengers
are present; the sun is strained in space,
                                an emptiness
in which he inches open like a paper sack

4:10

                                the eyes
divide the distance to, the distance into
and through the window where the surface swirls
against the glass:
                the face
is faded, pitted and unglazed
in places like a pocket photograph;
we sit too close
                together in
the shaken seats; the surface is
a stubbled blur of stones, a changeless face,
a white expanse

                    in which
a highway sign is winding with
a fence, a field, a farm; we sit too close
together in
                    the shaken seats;
the eyes: the eyes do not relieve me
of an alien greyness in their gaze; the deep,
the deepened ache
                    of them
5:15

a horizon is an ordinary line:
                              we overtake
a lantern at a gate, dragging the danger
in a warning through the loosened soot,
the interrupted streets, the shaken yards
into the silence and escape;
                              the red remains
behind the stores; windows, doors
in which the passage of a train is panoramic
and opaque:
              a sky
pales or fades, a grey dissolve
in which the distance is a wall

THE GREEN BEGINNING

There is something suspicious about the spring
for all of its intense, open preciousness.
The bitter impurities of winter are never
quite frozen altogether. Consider them:
the rusted burners, the shriveled unpicked vegetables,
the half-thawed dog-do.
There is something suspicious about the spring for all
of its lusciousness, tender and wet.

What we are certain of is the excess
of the wild onion in the grass,

and dill and mustard seed among the moderate,
the self-sufficient spinach and cabbages.
There is a relish of smells and of smells withheld
in the garden where grackles strut and stuff
their irridescent selves, and rabbits with
their wide ears and high fevers
have come to forage for the morning.

The sudden growth goes unnoticed even though
it amasses at the tips of things.
Too late we reach the birdbranch and the bobble
when the bird with its split, drop and whistle
has flown. Were we to follow, we would meet
the lowered worm and the fastened spider
within the shady places. We are aware of what
is extra like the shrike, the toad,
the tick, but in our own swollen moment
or afflatus, we miss most of it.

It is spoiled, the spring, at the very beginning a host
to wilt, mildew and blight. It is never
to be refulgent, replete. What is replenished
is diminished instantly by an understrata
of the famished, the crawling, the small. It is rottenness,
revival or rut: it is the fatal vine
on the lichened stump; it is the persistent itch of the
          sparrows
when they buffet and couple their stippled and dotted
ovaries and genitals; it is the companions of the plant,
the peony, when it opens with ants. The green
beginning is the eaten edge of the spring.

FIELD WITH FIGURATIONS

Whatever lies panting on its side
is spent. Flyblown, the meated breath is vile

and deadly in the prickled dirt. Silken
and lined with white, it has never been so prim
or flowerlike, the hairclip of an ear
which weeps a liquid sweetness to the air,
and quivering, the honey-sipping butterflies
above the homely meadow specked with daisies
now bobble in the quiet, fan and dry
with wings which blink the light in the heat of the day
from the junkyard on the hill; crusted and eased,
an effluvium as new as mucous dries.

The wind is warm. It winnows through a thousand
seeded heads too feverish to thresh them;
it trims the tapered stems which lean and creak,
and fans to tatters in the sheaths. A slick
light slides beneath the shaven sides, the fringe
of weightless motion like a silver-coated tongue
which salivates among the scant, the bladed
grasses. The flies infect and pucker. Blackbodied,
sacked and pinched, they deposit and abuse
while each egg in its fester larvates and chews
without a sound. The sun is sightless like
a whitened eye, a lidless bulge and tick.

On its side and stricken, the fermenting field
is sweet and toxic in the sun. The milled
insects spin through the colorless noon, land
and pitch, grip and rasp on a frazzled end.
The gutted cache is spilled, and the hillside grins
amid the beetle legs, the daubed abdomens
which pick at the coarse-grained, close stalks
and freckle them. The littered sod goes soft
with a strained and pallid wine. The smart and reek
of sodden boards and clotted roots; the smoke
among corroded pots now folds to seethe
beamless and larded, and strangles in the breeze.

D A V E S M I T H , *born in 1942, was educated at the University of Virginia, Southern Illinois University, and Ohio University. He spent four years in the U.S. Air Force, and he teaches now at Western Michigan University. His second collection of poems,* The Fisherman's Whore, *was published in 1974, and his poems and stories have appeared in such journals as the* Southern Review, *the* American Scholar, *and* The Nation.

HIGH ARE THE WINTER RIVERS

after Blood, Sweat & Tears

These things bear the brain's fruit:
the wheels of wind
            the sloping stones
            a forgotten sea
the way elder and ash dance
a prairie woman who makes love
like a wolf
            the high searing light
            the bed with edges coiled
like leaves stunned in ice. Believe
the mountainside where water falls
and goes on falling, that crystalline
            chandelier of air,

and on the flattest land, candescent,
the woman in you must burn again and again
the fleece of her lover's thigh,
like a wolf
rising toward winter rivers.

    The Dustman was right: poetry makes nothing
    happen. A poem, however, gnaws loose
    the leg crying in the dark,
    draws a regenerative circle
    and invites fish, lover, wolf, stone, and tree
    to come in and begin heart's music.

(A Story)

A wolf's paws may be tender of a season
but she knows where to walk, and goes
up under the tall manly trees
alone with her bright teeth
in the glacier's scars
and she is drinking, drinking
the icy mist
because it is right, because

she is a bruised woman
on the dry dirt, breathing a little hard,
hearing the current break against roots
like a dulcimer song, and in her heart
as in a poem, a man is rising, his breath
blooming throughout the cold high night
as he stains the earth under elder and ash,
and turns, circling on her scent.

THE CLOSET

The skull closes like a closet
ah, but the black air remains so lucid
like the stillness of living prairies
it keeps the long coats of fathers
the white silk robe of the morning
so many worn shoes canted and bent
leather cracked like a creek bed

who is this dark child that comes
each year to fit its tender body
into something bigger, older

are you the one who today feels
the hand fall limp
on the brass knob

when everything fits
when everybody walks out and wind
flees the arroyo and the last drop
of the river burns a rattler's tongue,
when the skull closes like a closet?

PIETAS: THE PETRIFIED WOOD

An old cottonwood has jeweled, my piece
the bruise of a warrior's first spear
hurtled, retrieved as the sun circles
and a boy hardens to a man.
I touch it to see him learn the art
of killing, and a man grows
to a boy in the presence of scars.

It does not live, on my desk,
in its warm grains, would not burn
though it is filled with smoke,
or slowly bear the agonizing green
of a desert spring. But as heartwood
I keep it for its weight, its shape
showing where the lance entered
and currents of sap loosed, shone,
broke the winter bark each year

as a man and a boy run down an arroyo
illusory with heat, tufts of dust
growing under their feet, the haze
of spring spreading like a sweat.
My finger sees the spear cocked
up like a bird toward the horizon
and I know his angle is still wrong
where a man grins up at the light
leaves, his arms open as if to soar,
and I feel the gouged bark fall, and
fall again, already beginning to be
mine, a spice in the hot dry air.

A . G . S O B I N , *born in* 1944, *is presently teaching at the University of Utah while on leave from the creative writing program at Wichita State University. He is coeditor of* Ark River Review, *and his poems have appeared in numerous magazines, including* Poetry, Beloit Poetry Journal, Poetry Northwest, Kansas Quarterly, *and* Iowa Review.

THE DECEMBER SKY

I examine my wound
disinterestedly

hold things in my hand
too shocking to see
or to throw away.

My life's too short
for wading and the town
circulates with paychecks
& misunderstanding.

Through my telescope
I watch a tintype of me
reclining nude
on the cold edge of space.

THE JANUARY SKY

The mare, dead since November, is still
on its side in the field of corn stubble,
the result equally of local custom
and the lack of a thaw
since the first hard freeze.

One ear is cupped to the ground filling
like a seashell with the vibrations
and rales made by the town
three miles to the south
dying in its sleep.

(When the truck comes in late March
they will have to peel up a layer of sod
to get all the body)

All night, the raised ear like radar
gathers complaints of animals
against life and the cold while
frost makes its trap out of the tangled mane
coating each hair like a brittle needle —
moonlight, entering, cannot escape
but reflects through the maze
until all its energy is spent and it
is drained off down the deep roots
of the hair into the milk of the neck.

The beam from the cracked purple eye
is locked on the one blank spot in Pegasus
that moves each night toward spring like
a black truck across the ice of the January sky.

MARCH RITE: GETTING IT UP

Spring in Iowa comes in three days
unfreezing the horse turds
steaming loose all the smells

of fields and drying barn wood
obscuring the skeletons in the trees
of last autumn's ill-fated kites
or last century's ill-fated negroes
softening up the highway's animal dead
for the winter to give up to the
slow, yellow-orange carcass trucks.

And the rasping sounds of the workman's
shovel scraping the fur from the concrete
repeats itself.
And the obscene expressions on
the deflated opossums is always the same.
AND the kinds of dead dogs
even begin to repeat them-
selves (in three-year cycles OR

maybe it's just every three miles
on the highway).
And the cupped yellow bulb-flowers poke up
through the snow in their usual fashion
to surprise us "so much" by their
mere presence in "all that winter"
but, on second thought,
they *do* look sort of dangerous and,
as always, we remark:
"too much like warheads!"

So we rush inside to the safety of drinks
and movies — worn-out silent films, our lives
repeating themselves — Chaplin & Keaton breathless
chasing, being chased, running north speeding south,
tattering across the hot teeth of projector gears,
shredding, curling high into the air, being driven on
by the projector, floating, at times almost motionless . . .
This is all film I have watched before!
I shut my eyes. I try to remember the outcome
of *The Secret War of the Eskimos*.
I could grow hard trying to remember.

D A V I D S T E I N G A S S *was born in Chardon, Ohio, in 1940, and grew up on a poultry farm. At eighteen he tried to leave the Midwest for good and spent ten years in Maine, Louisiana, and California, but "nothing worked." He is now an associate professor of English at the University of Wisconsin–Stevens Point. He and his wife Susan Eliot Ross, a lawyer-in-training, have one son, Brook Trout. His second book of poems,* American Handbook, *was published by the University of Pittsburgh Press in 1973.*

SONGS

1 *Song of the Arrowhead*

Lodged in a flake of bone
hundreds of years. Shoveled up by you
in a buckeye tree's roots.
$\qquad$ How
you would like to know.

How well
I am preserved.

2 *Song of the Chinese Goose*

I weed strawberries clean
never touching fruit or plants.
My body is carved
white foam, my legs and bill
bright orange paraffin.
My neck is a tight string of beads
you may stroke. My head
hangs in air, like the knotted tip
of an Indian's rope.
$\qquad$ Hypnotized,
I stand behind the mirror
of my still red eye:
$\qquad\qquad$ press your lips
$\qquad\qquad$ to the warm May apple
$\qquad\qquad$ of my forehead.

3 *Song of the Corn Kernels*

The soil clouds over.

We'll return, one
warm June night.
                            You'll hear
a flurry of buds: thirty thousand
leafy frogs
pop through the brown sky,
unfold and
gleam under moonlight.

4 *Song of the Dairy Cow*

I graze and drip sweet milk,
content all year,
                            except
when I come in heat
                            and
when green corn-ears show,
the slow mindless drool
begins. I'll leave
for a swollen, aching belly.

5 *Song of the Elm*

One big moma
I stroll among crazy quilts of bees
and the grab bag-nests
orioles hang out each spring.
My classic hourglass body
wanders in to open fields for lost weekends,
poison ivy roping the dizzy slant of my belly.
Sprigs of cloud trickle through my head. Clouds
and me, nudgers, wanting to be each other.

One shagbark hickory
leers around his odd, fenced-in corner.
He dreams of discovering toe room
in the flying Dutchman's boots
who wants to bring me down.

JAMES TIPTON, *born in* 1942, *lives with his wife and children on a farm near Elwell, Michigan, where he writes and raises sheep; he also teaches English at Alma College. His poems, short stories, and reviews appear regularly in magazines, including* Esquire, The Nation, South Dakota Review, Carolina Quarterly, Contemporary Poetry, *and* Field.

WINTER IN ELWELL

Those buffalo, white, that gather in the bean field, is it because of the winter? Heads down, they huddle together, eating the weather, swelling, exploding back into snow. No. Those were not buffalo. Giant birds. Those giant birds that gather in the bean field, why are they restless, why are they moving up and down, wings bursting out of their bodies in every direction? That woman, that woman in the bean field, why is milk rushing out of her breasts, out of her body, breaking over the field? That snow, that white snow that gathers in the bean field, what is that white snow?

FEBRUARY I TURN OFF THE
PORCH LIGHT AND GO OUTSIDE

It is night and it is the ice storm. A car is moving toward Alma. I stare into the darkness where there are no roads. Those willow trees, covered with ice, I hear them. Shucks of corn piled in the garden, the peach tree, the pussy willow, I think they are still there, under the ice. It is very still. I think I will say one word, even my name, and the ice will shatter. No, I will not do that. It is no use. I love these trees in their sleeves of water. I nuzzle into the honeysuckle near the house. It has the taste of that well I had forgotten. I shake the bush wildly. I see now it is that same bush I knew in October.

NOW EVERYONE IS WRITING POEMS ABOUT INDIANS

American poets stick together. Now they are writing prose poems about Indians. They are tired of cardboard stars in buckets of old milk. Now paint rushes out of their faces. It gathers in pools around their bodies. They sit alone, deep in their rooms, hacking their desks to pieces, looking for poems. They have cut the eyes out of the darkness to make light. Their pockets are stuffed with eyes. They do not want the darkness. They want to cry "Eureka!" But suddenly, on stolen ponies, they are pulled back into the darkness.

EXIT, PURSUED BY A BEAR

Tonight, the barn is sitting under the rain. I sit on the bed, thinking up rivers. Suddenly, rivers rush out of my eyes, flooding the room. I slosh through the dark to the kitchen. I do not want those rivers. I see now that the land has fallen out of the body. I want a dish of blueberries and beautiful women.

DIALOGUE

Damn poor guide you make.

ROY BRYAN

For you, I will be less desperate —
last night the sun
was a blood drop, perfect
in the early evening;
perhaps a giant god,
bleeding out of sight; or a woman,
young, again
beginning the world.

Forgive me, in the rain
the canoes have been taken —
the canoe house
in high water, gone.

I think in this weather
we are walking under
the water, hands
growing flat, into paddles,
or the wings of drowned birds.

The dead time will become a sleep,
and then a seed waking.
Somewhere it is north, a place
to go and be still.

PASTORAL

A shuddering geography pulls the dead sentences
through the body, and the spirit, that is destined
to be pure, says she is not here.

Slightly humiliated by the roses
that still want to gather under the eyes, I extend kisses,
at midnight, to the salt of her distant body.

I devour tea in sleep, and manuals of bright,
to tip the surface back to peace,
the ordinary, to light and quick devotions.

At a late hour, the sheep were calling to each other,
and I walked their narrow paths through clover,
calling over and over, for finer weather.

STEPHEN TUDOR *was born in Carroll, Iowa, in 1933. He teaches at Wayne State University in Detroit, commuting from Ann Arbor. He has published poetry in a variety of "little magazines," such as* Iowa Review, Anglo-Welsh Review, *and* North American Review, *and has also done some editing. Lately he has been writing poems about his uncle's farm in Van Buren County, Iowa.*

HAROLD

The voice in your chest speaks the language.
There is a storm over the barn or dust;
Please do your work or please lie down.
The gut-spirit may doze but never sleeps
That speaks in tones so low stones tremble.
What I say to you dies in the air.

The heart-spirit leads you to the past:
The silver opened your eyes to your life,
You spoke by father in the antique clock.
Give his voice to the church of the tree
Where the bell hangs. Let the sun go,
You will move when you have to.

Matter stares at space as dry as space.
Knives and ice are all the same —
The one long word you hear until you die.
Tell the grocer we'll bring apples Friday.
You are a hillside to mosquitoes.
Change your skin before morning comes.

The road turns to the left at Crown Hill.
Beyond's the barn, pasture, orchard, timber:
I saw a water snake breasting the river.
The mud voice of farms calls like birds;
Three part or two part, animal, shadow,
You go on and I go on the same.

THE AUGUR

He said everything is a struggle.
The corn is at war with the corn.
The barn blooms and withers.

Look at him. He is a string
In tune with the phone wires.
This man's mind will wander.

I say you have to be careful.
The rake or hoe may break off.
The sky is the same old sky.

He said nothing ever dies down.
Cows and chickens come from grain.
Grain comes from dirt and rain.

Nothing wakes up either, he said,
Unless it goes up in smoke.
Not one word will stand alone.

I say no one can hear a tree
And nothing's alive in the pump.
A voice is merely a voice.

YOU HELD THE AIR

You held the air in the palm of your hand
And told me stories. "Wet these stones," you said.

"They come from the creek." We stood in the shade
Of the dull moon. There was only the feel

Of tools and leather and to believe you
The rose by the steps would leap into snow.

I could not pin you down to flesh and bone.
The baskets by the tree had ears for you.

Where you were heading away from the house
I thought could be the sleep of far people.

"Watch for signs of coal beyond the orchard . . ."
Not one mosquito from those times gone by

Will fly again. They are flat in the outcrop
And you are of the age that pierced the air.

POEM FOR NANCY

I
The foreign country of the river
Rising. You held back from gar
And turtle . . . tangle of bur and tree.

I may not make them my own.
This house is where I come from.
Branches quarrel in the wind.

You made a fire. Wings of light
Beat against the clearing's edge.
The flames held your two eyes locked.

Fear at my back. I believe,
Yet lose my sense in dark places:
Each long known thing takes shape.

In sleep you entered river stone
Tumbled upon stone; thrashing carp;
Murdering owl and toad in peril.

Night long half-sleep; I fix my
Bedside hatchet-hand to ward
Dream creatures from my several doors.

II

And you, light friend, that sat rocking,
That took wing, the motion that startled you
And left us stranded with your dying music
Was long in making. There is no telling
How fine the string was tuned that sent you;
Our cold eyes penetrate, for once, the fiery
Sheen the sun has cast upon the river.
We fall away from you, and all our gestures
Are shadows, and all our speech, that carried
From room to room, fades in the rush of waters.

III

Conversations may go nowhere.
We keep them up in hopes of learning.
Theme and counter-theme:
These ways lend purchase,
And the platform or stage
Draws the mind on.

I have learned to be devious.
To be devious is unworthy.
This poem is about me, Nancy,
Constructing a poem.
Some go one way, others another.
I have to think about myself.

WINTER MORNING

Young: Beyond the bell-post by the door
           More rain than snow. Tell how the pail
           Fills with milk and more you have done.
           Look in your daybook: high and low,
           Harvest, hunter's moon, the time gone
           Pleads for you — you will take your ease.

Old: Head leaned against the steaming flank;
           Cow-dreams. My bride stays warm in bed,
           Mice and swallows keep me, dogs lie down.
           Take care, I say. I know the work
           The long night closes up. The town's
           Noon siren wakes me to the life.

Young: Weathered bell, but a rust-onion
           For tongue. Sleet leaps the yard light, black
           To black. In solstice, you observe,
           Spring rows of trees: prune, thin, prop, pick,
           Tend them to save. Weather makes work,
           Long dark of morning strikes the spark.

Old: Length of wire to bell the man home.
           Why press? The bell was new. Fireflies
           Tamed the house-crowned hill the night
           We burned. This we placed on the stones:
           They died, my bride may turn and wake
           For damp and chill. The dark lies still.

Young: Belled cows wind down that other day.
           Late wed you face the dark unkind.
           "Who will look after us?" For, once
           Stone long day comes to bed thin mates,
           Peace will not do. Tell the cows how
           Cool the life is — speak up to them.

Old: By the yard light, barn to house, lie
Water and snow. The milking's done,
The porch-cool cream will top the pails.
Those days are gone, all told, that lit
The air with a brass blaze. This new
Will come, now the sun rises late.

Both: How can you live in this slow time?
The dark way of December, starlit,
Stormed, keeps the fire in the range,
And the work ending, day comes down.
The bell rings true this year as last
That hangs on the post by the door.

ALBERTA TURNER, *born in* 1919, *is an associate professor of English at Cleveland State University and the director of the poetry center there. She also serves as associate editor of* Field, *and is the author of* Learning to Count (*University of Pittsburgh Press,* 1974). *She lives in Oberlin, Ohio.*

WRISTS

Asked me to be a woman:
      didn't mind
      swelled
      grew fine hair
      (you can braid fine hair to hang an anvil on)
      oiled my hands.

Asked me to make a god:
      couldn't do it.
      God was already grease
      a warm grease shaped like a rug you could
      stand on and be gone.

Asked for bread:
      couldn't do that either.
      So I said that bread was doom. I said their gums
      were sore and I rubbed
      their gums.

Then they asked how it felt to lean:
      so I took them one tide forward and one
      tide back, showed them that rock was red only
      if wet, showed how cattle doubled when they stood
      knee-deep, how the fence went back as far as
      the road, and grass
      was salt.

"Kinder," they begged,
          so I put on socks
          and felt for the ground through moss,
          showed them how fish spit out my hook,
          and how, when I lay under fish, they gaped
          and waved.

Then they grinned and shook and broke my hands off.

How explain to the finned a narwhal drowned? To the hoofed
a sand-dollar split?

So I offered wrists and they took
my wrists.

SISTERS

There were always five
                              or three or seven
cut out of brown paper
and joined at the skirt or curls,
with the same nose, the same lunch
pail. They had separate beds, but the same
lunch.

Being one, you took little things,
her seat next the teacher, *her* turn.
You put them back, but you owed.

If you tripped, one hauled you up;
if you died, you left them your babies, your old
cat, Mother's knives. But mostly
you stood
while one pinned.

STRUCTURE

I told you to make me some crazy
sandwiches and build me a crazy
house, hoping you'd open the door
and say, "Beer and sandwiches on the countertop."

So you built the house, round, lapped with off-white
tape. "Pull the end," you said, "and come
in. The sandwiches are terrible. I made
one with fangs and it's eating
the rest." And you jerked back and the tape stuck.

So I'm climbing around
and my teeth and nails have pulled every inch
and I know the thing's hollow because it jerks and bulges
and I can hear the cry of sandwiches, the horrible
moist cry of sandwiches
the shuddering fear of live sandwiches
and I can't get in.

TO LEONARD AND KERSTIN, WITH A GIFT OF BOOKS

Because your love uncurled my anxious toes,
Because you *were* your hospitality,
Let me return a portion of yourselves.

Your tactful clock tock-tickled my repose,
Your blanket hummed, your footed bathtub steamed
To help your love uncurl my anxious toes.

Your soup and Scotch leaned toward me from their shelves,
Your car gorged and disgorged me faithfully.
Let me return a portion of yourselves.

Sapphire brought her mouse and licked my nose,
Matthew told secrets, Eleanor whirled in glee
To watch your love uncurl my anxious toes.

Though books can't purr or pour, they mutter spells,
Spell dark secrets, speak rich recipes
When you accept a portion of yourselves.

So here is mead and mast and mistletoe,
Here's pickled prose and metric frumenty
Because your love uncurled my anxious toes
And mine returns a portion of yourselves.

MICHAEL VAN WALLEGHEN *was born in Detroit, Michigan, in 1938, and was educated at Wayne State University and the University of Iowa. He has taught at Wichita State University, and is presently an assistant professor of English at the University of Illinois. In 1966 one of his poems was awarded first prize in the annual Borestone Mountain Poetry Awards. Van Walleghen is the author of* The Wichita Poems *(Stonewall Press, 1973).*

POEM FOR MY GREAT GRANDFATHER

It snowed hard
that whole long winter.
At Eagle Harbor, Mohawk,
Calumet, the mines
and lumber camps
all closed. Mother
still remembers that,
and children starving,
diphtheria, lice. One night
her little sister died
and the next,
in that pitch black
beyond the last house
that ends her memory
of that town, the lake
that never freezes
froze. It looked,
I think, something
like the sky
above Detroit
on payday nights,
fridays, when the moon,

occasional, looked always
like the moon
of absent fathers —
white, varicose,
bulging like a fetus,
or like the eye
of some lumberjack
cheapskate drunk
dying on the ice.

ROBERT VAS DIAS, *born in 1931, is a graduate of Grinnell College. He is presently poet-in-residence and tutor at Thomas Jefferson College in Allendale, Michigan. His most recently published book of poems is* Speech Acts & Happenings *(Bobbs-Merrill, 1972), and his work has appeared in such magazines as* The Nation, The New Yorker, Mulch, Partisan Review, Poetry Review *(England), and* Sixpack.

SALVAGING SPIKES

That old nineteenth-century hold
of the creosote-soaked
tie makes me sweat
down on the railbed by
the side of the river: not
the spikes' rarity, but the use
I have in mind for them
as tent pegs, makes me work, whereas
you: what is it you are
on the track of, have you
caught some of my salvaging
fever to use Iron Horse artifacts
in our century (the link survives
as nostalgia, the rails
long since trucked off
down the valley to the nearest smelter
& the only rides you ever took in
your 5½ years, special excursions to nowhere,
but always of scenic interest);
there are just a few broken & seemingly
rotten ties scattered about & down
the embankment; I have found
a heavy piece of coupling hardware
with which to pound a spike like a chisel
to free the one embedded in
the perfectly preserved inside wood; the sound is

wonderful, an anvil sound, a railroad
gang, ringing sound, it is
certainly a nineteenth-century sound, I have
visions of doing a long day's toil
for meager wages, already my back
muscles ache, my wrist numbs, & you
sitting on the ground watching this furious
labor, getting tired, bored,
hungry, not fired
by enthusiasm, or mania,
keep asking: — Papa, when are we going back? —
& I answer: — Just one more
spike & we'll have enough — then that
urging holds me back
from salvaging more,
your limits of patience & endurance
met, though I could go on
hunting past supper, past sleep, past
the turn of the century, across the wreckage of
this country filled with the cast-off
artifacts of dreams.

AN IMPOSSIBILITY

Driving along the eastern shore of Lake Michigan
tonight unconsciously I punch the AM
radio station-selector-button for
our usual station this time an hour later
in New York City where we both consciously
at this time wish we were, when be —
hold! — we have punched in to a tropo-
spheric rendition of the crappy early fifties
big-band music, making us dance close with
other partners long before we knew each other:
those godawful hits I never knew
the names of!, could never on the airwaves avoid

hearing, as tonight, sloppy at even 800 miles they seek us
out, those tunes of drawn-out adolescent anguish and
embarrassment to remind us of
what we always never and sometimes were.

PETOSKEY STONE

On the lake-bottom near
the shore it appears to move
among others, it is shiny when I lift it
out of the water & contains many
small shapes within
its remarkable one: each
shape is its own particular
4-sided, 5-sided, 8-sided cell, the smaller
wedged at regular intervals between
the larger; edges of the polygons are
serrated like those of sea shells but
smooth & each has a spot at its center, a liver spot:
edges, spots, the small universes
fade from the heat on my hand, become
a speckled, dusty gray
stone with little character. It needs
that water to live between
two oceans. In my house there are
many such stones.

REX VEEDER, *born in* 1947, *teaches in Lincoln, Nebraska. His work has been accepted by a number of magazines, including* Quartet *and* Dragonfly, *and he has published one volume of poetry. He lends a hand in the publication of* Pebble *and* Saltillo *magazines.*

MAGIC

It is hunter's magic to perform,
confuse acting with death
to grow arrows from painted hands
or rock, or spears that
shoot like whittled roots into throats
bringing down giants:
birds, buck, bear.

There is magic in confusion
not being there
to escape chains, or vanish
under ice in a river
to sleep in a box wrapped with rope
in a dark hole to wriggle out
to a surface lit like a moon.
Bodies may be cut in half,
or fire crammed in your throat
dulling tissue until
you can swallow a sun.

Let alone miracle,
there is the magic of healing;
bent bones become oak
sickness flows like wind from hot bodies
or the soothing of jumping muscles
reveals the release of pain.

There is mountain magic
high enough to drown fire
with clouds like steam from coffee.
Standing on one leg
you can let the sun have your eyes
bloom visions, sweat rivers
never move except your hair
tangling about your face
holy, fragile, the texture of fire.
There is the consuming of yourself
feeding on the mountain until
there is no leaving.
There is no element you cannot be
when you are high enough
not to want to leave the ground.

MY SON . . .

With the slightest sound
you are shattered.
I see your face as liquid,
your mouth moves to taste our foreign water.
You huddle, as though pushing through slow rivers
to find a word — *gurgle, lob,* and
fear stands in your pants
its legs churning.

I know
you felt napalm
as you ran in that rain
flashing like a neon sign,
while I hunted pheasant
in cornfields trenched with snow

so I confess
I search your face for wounds.
I see you are hungry.
You have grown thin,
traveled thousands of miles on your stomach.
I will fatten you up.

Come, though you are not easy to explain
I suggest to our friends
it's like the pines in high, sharp air.
They are thin, tangled in rock
there above tree line
they make pain a novelty
tourists can take home.

MARK VINZ *was born in North Dakota in* 1942, *grew up in Minneapolis, Minnesota, and Shawnee Mission, Kansas, and attended the universities of Kansas and New Mexico. He has published poems in such magazines as* South Dakota Review, The Nation, West Coast Poetry Review, Kansas Quarterly, *and his first collection of poems,* Winter Promises, *has just been published by BkMk Press. He currently teaches English at Moorhead State College in Minnesota, and edits the poetry magazine* Dacotah Territory.

VARIATIONS ON A THEME

1

This morning
my child dances naked
in front of the mirror,
unashamed,
unafraid of growing old.
Her face is as thin
as her breakfast egg shell,
looking toward me
huddled between bedsheets.
When she leaves the room
the image keeps dancing
in the mirror.

2

Important decisions today:
clean sheets, the price
of hamburger, where the line
is to be broken,
how to continue.
At the supermarket
I watch a woman beat her child
with a package of celery.

He has broken a jar of applesauce,
while dancing in the aisles.

3

This evening there are fireworks
and dancers in the park.
Behind the crowd,
the old ones
who will not leave their benches
clap their hands together,
even though they cannot see,
even though they cannot be heard.

NORTH DAKOTA GOTHIC

The farm was abandoned
nearly three months ago.
Someone has stolen the mailbox,
the roofless house still reeks of smoke.

Beside the road,
a field of sunflowers
leans against the frost
like some vast forgotten army,
heads down and waiting.

Across a bare elm branch
the wind brings news of early snow.

FOR THE FAR EDGE

When I leave this place
I will have too much baggage —
there is always too much,

and not enough.
Songs without singing,
memory without blood.

No one will believe the winters,
the land as flat and broad
as God's own shinbone,
where nordic stormtroops
wring the manna from the earth
and build the towns
whose shadows stretch for miles.

No one will believe the poets —
poets singing in the sunflowers,
poets in buffalo robes
dancing on tiptoe in their own hair,
Martin Luther and Buddha
swimming naked in the Red River.

Traveler, accept what you will —
I could never conjure this.

JAMES L. WHITE *was born in Indianapolis, Indiana, in 1936, and lives now in Minneapolis, Minnesota. His first book of poems,* Divorce Proceedings, *was published in 1973 by the University of South Dakota Press, and a second collection is forthcoming. Because of his long affiliation with tribal people, he was chosen as guest editor for a special Native American issue of* Dacotah Territory. *He is at present the resident poet for the Saint Paul (Minnesota) Council of Arts and Sciences, Poets in the Schools program.*

ANDERSON, INDIANA

It all fails now:
porch gliders begin
as he takes the last rim shot into dusk,
as moths rise in suicide against the reading lamp,
as the locust cries forever,
as the weathercock rusts forever,
as heat lightning reveals the blue bike on rainless nights.

I drink to the town's death
by a granary of broken windows screaming into the night,
where our last drunk Indian was run visionless to the town's
    edge.

A drunkard from the window fan,
mystery magazines and diner food,
sitting in this appointed darkness by the depot
where once cried the great trains
extinct by my boyhood's end.

MOVER

I move each fall
past a summer burning.
Remember the roans in Billy Red's field.

Rent's higher in town.
The borrowed chair
and Navajo stuff where I used to live.
Jim Polston's picture with John Wesley
and David's toy of the tumbling man.

Everything's on shelves just right:
Lorca,
my corduroy
and straw angels from Juarez.

Just found a 24 hour diner
and scratch paper to say hello,
that I made it back fine
with enough left
for a new winter coat.

MINNEAPOLIS WHITE CASTLE, WINTER '72

Old and longhairs in crome light.
Coffee drinkers, bus waiters.
Holy tumblers of time . . .

. . . who once from earth rooms
or painted bird ships
nodding in coves as elders at noon.

A freak plays The Stones . . .

. . . who danced bulls then,
or painted warring blue
in Northern white fur and iron.

What wino's ancient father . . .

. . . lifted prayer doves,
followed the entrail's direction
towards a foreign drop of bright earth?

Some Memphis dung beetle loses time
falling dead to the White Castle floor.

Our 6-A pushes dimly through snow.
We board with a Crete Mother's sea song
forged under our common skin.

DAY SLEEPER

Under Seconal
my apartment diminishes in shafts of dusty light.

Nearly there
something hangs unforgiving above this bed,
towards me,
my people,
and theirs into the hills.

A day sleeper now,
I shatter neon into morning stars,
above the arms of bridges,
the blasted rock,
smoke and time.

NATHAN WHITING *was born in* 1946, *grew up in Illinois, and has lived in Oklahoma, Iowa, and New York. His most recent book is* Transitions (*Seven Woods Press*).

MARIJUANA PATCH ON THE STATE
HOSPITAL'S FORMER GROUNDS

Too green. Too green.
The old stalks are rope.
Underneath mad, old, suicided patients,
heroin addicts caught fighting the myths
of innocent rural America
are under white stones beside the stream.
Grow little weeds.
Become plant sex rosin
in the sun broken shade.
No insects.
No fires.
So green.
The steers will gain 2½ pounds every day.
If they stomp on Kevin Armbrust
who imagined he tied a bale of hay with his intestines
it would mean nothing,
but don't let them eat the marijuana.
I used to play naughty games naked
hidden by leaves like this
under the tallest cottonwood in the state.
Green green.
I have no matches.
Become brown, grow seeds
and I will burn you
when I get high.

GOOD-BY ON AN ALL DAY BEAN PLANTER

In my life there will be U.S. famine.
My strength has worked into the land.
My fertilizer neck.
My wood spray ears.
My bug killing toes are done.
The nation's energy has passed through me.
I piddled it out.
I lost a herd of steers
to an asbestos commercial.
I plowed the hill tops.
I hid a year's corn in a gopher
to plead bankruptcy.
Sell me to the labor exchange backwards
and feed my duck.

ROBLEY WILSON, JR., *born in* 1930, *teaches at the University of Northern Iowa, and is editor of* North American Review. *His poems have appeared in the* Atlantic Monthly, The New Yorker, The New Republic, Esquire, *and a number of literary quarterlies.*

AT NIGHT

It is day's end; I am thinking of weight—
how heavy I feel, how my flesh and my bones
having stayed alight so many hours are gone
all solemn like a cat slinking into a room.
The moon is outside the window, waning again;
it sits on its haunch in a circle of weather.
Tonight I am no brighter than the moon,
I only remember being silver and prophetic,
I move with no more haste than dark does.

Weight, I said. I find in you the pretense
of the moon—how you seem a center weathers
cleave to, how you assume a distant influence,
diminish but never fall, how you will not quite
disappear in the blackest night I invent you.
Instead—look—I am the one sinking, the one
worn, the one who feels even the moon's age
as near as the window it lights. Dull gravity—
tonight a thousand moons won't make me flow.

And at morning when this moon low in the west
looks to be etched in glass, then it will twin
you and be like half a dream. I may not bear
the weight of you, you are all a coursing on
the Zodiac from one sterile sign to the next,
you are the sea creature I cannot begin to coax
to the lap of the earth—whose close approach
would heave up houses. This is an invention of
bodies and forces, of fatigue and living alone.

WARREN WOESSNER, *born in* 1944, *lives in Madison, Wisconsin, where he works as a medicinal chemist and edits* Abraxas. *A full-length collection of his poetry,* Landing, *has been published by Ithaca House.*

NAVAJO POEM

The old man
sits
in the blue shade
of the coke machine.
All day,
tourists steal
his picture.
He has seen the gods
evicted
and the empty land
fill up with roads.
He has hocked
his bracelets
for a place
to rest,
and sold his rings
for peace.
Like water
in the sun,
he evaporates.
At last, the moon
lifts him out
into the painted night.
Friends are waiting.
Coyote sings
old songs.
In the cool sand,
snake
writes his name.

FLITCRAFT'S WOODS

The last seeds
are eaten. The birds, retreated
to the backyard feeders
or the pines upland. Leaves
fill up the tracks where raccoons
or possums pushed out for food.
Not a sound; ice has found
the last free water, and, too high to hear,
the vulture turning over us
veers off: below, just snow and trees,
and we're still moving.

LOST COUNTRY

Walking, I begin to notice
how the grass survives
between the houses,
how old the trees are.
The shape of the earth appears.
The hill still slopes down to the lake
despite the houses, poles, wires, roads.
I see how it was
after the glacier melted,
how the stones settled down.
One good look
and all our work is gone.

Once I found a deserted street
buried in the woods, broken
by roots.
Virginia creeper and wild onion
pushed out from the cracks.
Branches met down the middle
of "Capitol Avenue."
It was good to see.
If we leave our footsteps
they don't have a chance.

ABOUT THE EDITOR

Lucien Stryk's five books of verse include *Notes for a Guidebook* (1965), *The Pit and Other Poems* (1969), and *Awakening* (1973), which received the Society of Midland Authors Poetry Award in 1974. His poems and essays have appeared in anthologies and periodicals, he has received prizes in poetry competitions, and he has held a National Endowment for the Arts grant in creative writing and a National Translation Center grant to translate Zen poetry. He is editor of *World of the Buddha*, and translator, with Takashi Ikemoto, of *Zen: Poems, Prayers, Sermons, Anecdotes, Interviews; Afterimages: Zen Poems of Shinkichi Takahashi;* and *Zen Poems of China and Japan: The Crane's Bill*. He has given poetry readings throughout the United States and England, has been a visiting lecturer in Japan and Iran, and presently teaches at Northern Illinois University.